PR

ENVISION THE LIFE

Jesus charged his disciples to do one main thing – to make disciples. Unfortunately, the church (all of us) are too often distracted by good things and overlook the priority of living as disciples and making new disciples who will then make disciples. In his book *Envision the Life*, Dr. Michael Dean gives us biblically solid and practically effective guidance for that journey. His desire is to awaken us to see, to picture, the abundant and joyful life of a Christ-honoring disciple. He then clearly describes seven attributes that fill out that picture of the journeying follower of Jesus. This book can be a guide for the new believer, a reminder and challenge for the long-time Christian, a study guide for a discipleship group, or a curriculum for a larger group. I plan to return to it again and again to help me stay focused on Jesus.

Terry Coy
Director of Missions
Southern Baptist Convention of Texas

While the twentieth and early twenty first century produced many church attenders I fear we have not produced many disciples—disciplined followers of Jesus Christ. For that does not happen simply be attending a service, a conference or an event...or by listening to a pod cast, reading a book or following a blog, as good as those things may be. It happens by the investment of life into life, and that takes time, intentionality and persistence. Mike Dean nails what it takes, how to do it, and the rewards it brings. So if you want to increase your legacy for the future and impact for today you'll want to read this book. And what's really important—I've watched the man live what he's written. So you won't be reading theory but authentic life change. So, what are you waiting for?!

Dr. Bob Reccord
President/CEO Hope for the Heart
Plano, Texas

It is an honor to recommend Dr. Michael Dean's new book *Envision the Life*. From the very start Dr. Dean's words are powerful, profound and inspiring. The book is set up in a simple and practical way for believers of all stages. I look forward to taking groups of people through it in the near future.

Cliff Lea
Senior Pastor
First Baptist Church
Leesburg, Florida

In *Envision the Life*, author and pastor Michael Dean provides foundational guidance to living the life of a disciple. His theme of envision carries through the book as the key concept we as disciples should "live out" as a life which God desires for those in fellowship with Christ. As you read this book...envision living solely and completely devoted for Christ.

Kenneth Priest
Director of Convention Strategies
Southern Baptists of Texas Convention

Dr. Dean unlocks the key component to assuring your dreams and visions become reality. The pivotal differentiation between your dreams becoming reality centers on whether or not your dreams are the dreams God envisions for your life. Dr. Dean provides his readers with a biblical approach in searching for God's vision. If you desire what God envisions for your life, read and apply the content in this book.

Eric Fuller
Eric Fuller Evangelistic Association, Inc.

Envision the Life reveals the heart of a disciple-making pastor who has led his large fellowship to focus on seven key formations for producing reproducers. Loaded with great scripture and action goals, it is a banquet of joy. I could not put down my fork!

Waylon B. Moore
Founder and President of Missions Unlimited, Inc.

As Pastor of Travis Avenue Baptist Church in Ft. Worth, TX, Dr. Michael Dean has stood in the leadership spotlight for more than twenty years. He has mentored countless seminary students and has effectively led his church. The principles shared in Envision the Life: Living in God's Unrelenting Vision for Your Life reflect his personal pursuit of Jesus. Dr. Dean speaks with authority challenging the matured disciple to reexamine his life against the truth of God's Word while laying a blueprint for the new believer to follow so that he might become an effective Christ follower. This book will challenge every Christian to focus all of their life on Jesus and Jesus alone.

Dr. Brad McLean
Senior Pastor
First Baptist Church
New Braunfels, TX

ENVISION THE LIFE

LIVING IN GOD'S UNRELENTING VISION FOR YOUR LIFE

Michael D. Dean

Envision the Life:
Living in God's Unrelenting Vision for Your Life

Published by Rainer Publishing
www.rainerpublishing.com

ISBN 978-0692426197

Printed in the United States of America

CONTENTS

Acknowledgments 11

Introduction 13

Part I ~ Envision ... The Life 25

    Part I ~ Day 1: The Gospel of Discipleship 27

    Part I ~ Day 2: Follow Me! 33

    Part I ~ Day 3: The Progress Process 39

    Part 1 ~ Day 4: Following Jesus into Life 45

    Part I ~ Day 5: Don't Miss the Life 51

Part II ~ Envision ... Learning The Truth Of God 57

    Part II ~ Day 1: The Condition of Your Heart 59

    Part II ~ Day 2: The Plan 65

    Part II ~ Day 3: The Profitable Word 73

    Part II ~ Day 4: Getting a Word from God 81

    Part II ~ Day 5: Memorizing and Meditating on God's Word ..89

Part III ~ Envision ... Obeying God 95

    Part III ~ Day 1: Obeying God 97

    Part III ~ Day 2: Self-Denial 103

    Part III ~ Day 3: Loving God vs. Loving the World 111

    Part III ~ Day 4: Training for Godliness 117

    Part III ~ Day 5: The Role of the Holy Spirit 125

Part IV ~ Envision ... Serving God And Others 133

Part IV ~ Day 1: Our Example in Service 135

Part IV ~ Day 2: Grace for Service 141

Part IV ~ Day 3: Unwrapping Your Spiritual Gifts 147

Part IV ~ Day 4: Getting an M.B.A....................................155

Part IV ~ Day 5: Great is Your Reward 161

Part V ~ Envision … Sharing Jesus Christ............................167

Part V ~ Day 1: God's Glorious Quest...............................169

Part V ~ Day 2: Partners with God 175

Part V ~ Day 3: With Great Boldness 181

Part V ~ Day 4: Starting Spiritual Conversations 187

Part V ~ Day 5: Finishing Spiritual Conversations...........193

Part VI ~ Envision … Living By Faith....................................201

Part VI ~ Day 1: Faith's Foundation..................................203

Part VI ~ Day 2: Accessing the Life...................................211

Part VI ~ Day 3: The Prayer of Faith.................................217

Part VI ~ Day 4: Suffering and Faith.................................225

Part VI ~ Day 5: Trust and Obey 233

Part VII ~ Envision … Honoring God In Worship................239

Part VII ~ Day 1: The True Seeker in Worship 241

Part VII ~ Day 2: So What is Worship?..............................249

Part VII ~ Day 3: Our Private Worship 255

Part VII ~ Day 4: Our Public Worship 261

Part VII ~ Day 5: Worship Changes Me 269

Part VIII ~ Envision … Building Christ-Centered Relationships.....277

Part VIII ~ Day 1: The Fellowship of the Three..............279

Part VIII ~ Day 2: Christ-centered Families.....................285

Part VIII ~ Day 3: Christ-centered Churches 291

Part VIII ~ Day 4: Membership Has Its Privileges...........297

Part VIII ~ Day 5: The "One Anothers"............................305

Conclusion 313

Endnotes..317

Acknowledgments

This book has grown out of the process of our church seeking to zero in on the mission Jesus gave His followers when He said, "Go and make disciples." Over a period of several months some key pastoral and lay leadership in our church combed through the Scriptures seeking to identify those qualities, characteristics and habits that typify a passionate follower of Jesus Christ. This process helped us develop what we have called the Blueprint for Spiritual Formation.

We asked the questions, "What kind of life does God have in mind for those who call upon Him? As Jesus endured the enormous sufferings of the cross, what exactly did He have in mind for those who would put their trust in His redeeming activity?" He said, "I have come that they might have life, and have it to the full" (John 10:10). So what is this "life...to the full"? I have an idea that most of us are living far short of the vision God had in mind for us when He sent His Son to die for our sins and to be gloriously raised from the dead.

I am indebted to Brad Waggoner for his great work done in *The Shape of Faith to Come*. Our Blueprint team knew that we were not trying to reinvent the wheel, and that many had written on the subject of spiritual formation in the church. Brad's seven "domains" of spiritual formation served as the foundation for the development of our Blueprint for Spiritual Formation, and consequently for this book.

I am privileged to serve the Travis Avenue Baptist Church that has been in the heart of Fort Worth, Texas since 1911. I am profoundly grateful that this established church continues to stretch itself to become all it needs to be to fulfill our Lord's mandate to make disciples of all nations in an ever-changing city and world. The team of staff members and church leaders, along with the family of church members are among some of my greatest friends in the world.

My wonderful assistant Jo Ann Morgan was of inestimable value in proofing and editing the manuscript for this book.

My greatest earthly joy is to be surrounded and supported by the love of my precious wife Nan, our daughters Allison and Ashley, their husbands Anthony and Chris, and our adored grandchildren Caroline, Cooper and Eleanor.

My prayer is that this book will be used by God to inspire a quest in the hearts of readers to become passionate, life-long followers of Jesus.

INTRODUCTION

In the movie *Bobby Jones: Stroke of Genius*, actor Jim Cavie-zel played the role of the legendary golfer Bobby Jones, who dominated the world of golf through most of the 1920s. The closing scene of the film had Jones, along with his friend and golf writer O.B. Keeler, driving into an open field overlooking rolling hills and beautiful trees just outside of Augusta, Georgia. Bobby got out of the car and stood in the knee-deep grass. He looked at Keeler and said, "We're standing on the first tee. I'm going to call it Augusta National." Bobby Jones saw more than grass, trees and hills. He envisioned a golf course, and not just any golf course. Jones envisioned the Augusta National Golf Club becoming one of the great golf courses of the world. In 1933 his vision became a reali-ty and to this day each year Augusta National hosts the Masters Tournament, one of the four major champion-ships of professional golf.

History is filled with stories of humanity's *fulfilled* vi-sions, but it also reveals even more of humanity's *failed* visions. The very year that Bobby Jones' golfing vision was achieved, Adolph Hitler became the Chancellor of Germany. He, too, was driven by an imposing vision. Hitler envisioned an entire world dominated by a "super race" of human beings who, through an evolutionary process, had rid themselves of any weak traits. To fulfill his vision Hitler began exterminating those groups that he considered "weak." Of course, this resulted in the horrific Holocaust that led to the deaths of more than six million Jews. For the first few years Hitler's vision of a world dominated by Nazism appeared to be succeeding. Other nations of the world, however, saw the evil in Hitler's vision and rose up to resist and ultimately defeat it. As powerful as Hitler had become, he was not able to sustain his quest and achieve his vision … and we're all grateful he didn't.

In fact, no human being will ever accomplish all they dream of accomplishing. This remains one of the more exasperating parts of being human … many of our hopes and plans remain just dreams that never come true. The old adage "if you can dream it you can achieve it" isn't always true. For a variety of reasons, what we envision for ourselves and for those we love often proves very illusive. We go to our graves thinking, "If only…"

But what if your dreams and aspirations are not just your own? What if your life's vision is linked to the vision of One whose dreams *always* come true … whose vision *always* comes to pass … whose purposes are *always* achieved?

The Bible reveals God as the One whose plans "stand firm forever, the purposes of his heart through all generations" (Psalm 33:11). The Lord Himself declares: "My purpose will stand, and I will do all that I please" (Isaiah 46:10).

The glorious truth of the gospel is that what God lovingly purposes for us in His Son Jesus Christ *will* be fulfilled. The Apostle Paul describes what God envisioned for us in salvation: "And we know that in all things God works for the good of those who love him, who have been called according to his purpose. For those God foreknew he also predestined to be conformed to the likeness of his Son, that he might be the firstborn among many brothers. And those he predestined, he also called; those he called, he also justified; those he justified, he also glorified" (Romans 8:28-30).

So God has in mind a glorious purpose for our lives. He predestined or predetermined that the ultimate outcome of our salvation would be that we would conform to the likeness of Jesus Christ. God's purposes *will* be achieved; this is the destiny of all followers of Christ. His vision *will* become reality. To that end God is working to bring to completion that glorious finished product of our salvation.

To affect this magnificent destiny for us God did three things. First, He *called* us (v.30). This means more than just being invited. When God calls us He summons us and enables us to come to Him. Second, God *justified* us (v.30). This is the great work of God where the righteousness of Jesus is credited to us, not based upon our good works, but upon the work of Christ on the cross. Third, God *glorified* us (v.30). In other words, our destiny is to one day stand before God completely perfected into the likeness of Christ in body, soul and spirit. Interestingly it is so certain that God's vision for us will be achieved that Paul speaks of it in the past tense, as though it had already occurred!

God has in mind this entire process when He calls us into a relationship with Himself through Jesus Christ, with the final product being human lives transformed into the likeness of Jesus. For some reason there's part of this process that God intends to happen in this life, otherwise He would take us straight to heaven when we are saved. This gives meaning to everything that happens to us in our earthly life … and everything we do. God is working them all together for good (v.28) … the heart-aches, the failures, the trials, the suffering, the adversity, all of it. Again, the "good" toward which God is working is shaping us into the likeness of His Son. In this lifelong process God is forming us and fitting us for heaven.

God envisions all of this from the beginning. It is not a wistful dream for Him; it is His resolute purpose to bring many sons and daughters to glory. It shall be so!

With that being the case, what sort of life did God the Father envision for us when He sent His Son Jesus into this world as the sacrifice for our sins? When Christ was hanging on the cross, dying for our sins, what kind of transformation did He envision happening in a person's life? When the Holy Spirit comes to dwell in an individual what sort of change does He envision?

The Triune God envisions a life that resembles the life of Jesus Christ. Jesus lived, died and rose again to reproduce in us the life that He lived while He was on this earth. Obviously there are aspects of Jesus' life that we will never be or do because He was the God/Man; but the gift of eternal life He gives certainly includes the possibility of our genuinely becoming like Him. When Jesus rose from the dead the Father intended to replicate that resurrection life in the lives of those who follow Jesus. "Just as Christ was raised from the dead through the glory of the Father, we too may live a new life" (Romans 6:4b).

In the events of the crucifixion, resurrection and ascension of Jesus, along with the gift of the Holy Spirit, God was enacting the plan by which eternal life would be made available to all who put their trust in Jesus Christ. God envisioned the forgiveness of our sins through the atoning sacrifice of Christ upon the cross (1 John 4:10). God purposed the resurrection of our mortal bodies when He raised His own Son from the dead, becoming the "firstfruits" of those who would be raised from the dead (1 Corinthians 15:20).

But is that all there is? Is that all that God had in mind when Jesus died on the cross and rose from the dead? Certainly those are great blessings for us … sins forgiven and heaven gained. If that is, indeed, all there is then certainly we would have reason to rejoice. If, however, we think that's all there is to the Christian life then we are experiencing only part of the life that God had in mind for us when He enacted the great plan of salvation.

Consider it in these terms: "(Jesus Christ) gave himself for us to redeem us from all wickedness and to purify for himself a people that are his very own, eager to do what is good" (Titus 2:14). Do you see it? Can you catch a glimpse of the deep change that God envisioned for us when He sent Jesus? Redeemed from wickedness? Yes, but more. Purified and cleansed from our sin? Absolutely, however it doesn't stop there. God envisions people who are His very own, unique, special people who have experienced such transformation that they now eagerly *desire* to do what is good.

This is the grand quest of God in our lives today, this very moment, and every second of every day: "Being confident of this, that he who began a good work in you will carry it on to completion until the day of Christ Jesus" (Philippians 1:6). It shall be accomplished!

So our lives are not yet complete. We are not yet ready for heaven, though our destination is certain. So what do we do? Do we sit idle and passive in this process? Absolutely not! In fact we are very active participants. "Continue to work out your salvation with fear and trembling, for it is God who works in you to will and to act according to his good purpose" (Philippians 2:12b-13).

That is what God is up to. He is working in you and me with a particular vision in mind. The life of a follower of

Christ is one in which we continue to work out our salvation. Notice we don't work *for* our salvation but we work it *out* … continually. We do it because of a greater reality … God is working in us to will and to act according to his good purpose. So we are to work *out* what God is working *in.*

Biblically speaking this process of God bringing us into such union with His Son that we are transformed into His likeness is called "discipleship." In more recent times it has been called "spiritual formation."

It all starts with vision. If somehow we might catch the vision of the fabulous life God has in mind for us we are on our way to the genuine life of a follower of Christ.

Dallas Willard, in his book *Renovation of the Heart,* gives a helpful illustration. Willard likens the process of spiritual formation to the process of learning a new language. To begin the process one must have some idea of what it would be like to speak this new language – what it would be like to move about in a different culture being fluent enough in the language of that culture to be able to order a meal in a restaurant, navigate through a train station or bargain for a good deal in a shop. If a person doesn't possess this vision they will likely never learn the new language. Willard states, "If the vision is clear and strong, it will very likely pull everything else along with it; and the language … will be learned, even in difficult and distracting circumstances." [1]

Willard goes on to explain that it does, however, require more than vision. It also requires the intention to pay the price of the sacrifice that needs to be made in order to learn a new language. Additionally it requires the knowledge of the means necessary for one to learn a new language ... attending language courses, listening to audio recordings of the language, hanging around with people who speak the language, etc. The same thing is true in spiritual formation or discipleship.

The fundamental business of the local church is to bring people into the fullness of the life in Christ. What does this look like? Many authors have sought to describe it in different ways. I am deeply indebted to the writings and research of the following authors in defining the primary attributes of a Christ-follower:

- Brad Waggoner in his book *The Shape of Faith to Come*
- Ed Stetzer and Thom S. Rainer in their book *Transformational Church*
- Eric Geiger, Michael Kelley and Philip Nation in their book *Transformational Discipleship*

Their collaborative work identifies at least seven foundational attributes of Christ-followers. My desire is dig down deeper into these attributes to assist readers in moving along the journey of spiritual formation and the life God envisions for us in Christ. These attributes are:

Introduction

LEARNING THE TRUTH – The primary tool of the Holy Spirit in spiritual formation is the Word of God. To grow in Christ we must be diligent students of the Word of God and have a hungry, teachable spirit.

OBEYING GOD AND DENYING SELF – God commands us to be obedient to Him in all things, which means we must deny self. When we follow His commands we show our love for Him. Our love for God and our obedience to Him are inseparable.

SERVING GOD AND OTHERS – Jesus came not to be served, but to serve and to give His life a ransom for many (Matthew 20:28). We grow spiritually when we live a life of service to God and to others in His name.

SHARING CHRIST – Jesus came to seek and to save the lost. God's strategy is to call, equip and send His followers into the world with His love and message of redemption. The Great Commission calls us to "make disciples *of all nations.*"

EXERCISING FAITH – This is a spiritual ability that undergirds everything else. It springs from our exposure to the truth. Without faith it is impossible to please God (Hebrews 11:6a). Through faith God uses ordinary people to do extraordinary things.

SEEKING GOD – God is a rewarder of those who diligently seek Him (Hebrews 11:6). Our pursuit and worship of God must be active and continuous. Our ultimate destiny in life is to glorify God.

BUILDING RELATIONSHIPS – Spiritual formation does not happen in isolation. God created us to be in an interactive relationship with Him and with others. In the context of those relationships we encourage one another toward spiritual growth.

This book is structured to hopefully assist you in exploring ways you can grow in each of these seven attributes of a disciple of Jesus Christ. If you wish you may make it a part of your daily devotional time by covering one section each week. Read a short chapter each day and meditate on its meaning in your own spiritual development. Each section begins with an invitation for you to envision what the purposes of God would look like fully operational in your life. I have suggested a passage of Scripture for you to read in preparation for each chapter. Also, each chapter is chocked full of Scripture references that you may want to take time to read for yourself in your copy of Scripture.

My prayer for you as you read this book is that God will awaken in you a vision of the incredible life God had in mind for you when He sent His Son to die on the cross and to be resurrected from the grave. I pray that you will grasp what God envisioned for you when, after Christ's resurrection, He ascended to the place of supremacy at the right hand of the Father in heaven, and then, from heaven, sent down His Holy Spirit to dwell in those who have put their trust in Christ.

Brad Waggoner, in his book *The Shape of Faith to Come*, invites us to use our imaginations:

"Imagine a church filled with believers who are spiritually alive, hungry for God, filled with wisdom, and living lives of impeccable character. Imagine a local community seasoned with Christians like this who truly desire to live as salt and light in the midst of their neighbors, coworkers, and friends. Wouldn't it be encouraging to know that the watching world would see a collective witness that reflects the truths of the gospel? Consider what it would be like if the majority of Christians shared the good news of Jesus regularly with those in their sphere of influence.

"What if your walk with God was consistently characterized by love, obedience, loyalty, praise, purpose, prayer, service and passion? Visualize the experience of feasting upon God's Word and having it captivate your thoughts, feelings, and perspectives. Contemplate the joy of knowing your life is bringing glory and pleasure to our eternal God.

"Consider living in a community of faith, the body of Christ, where fellow believers actually love, honor, respect, and care for one another. Think about what it would be like to be encouraged, admonished, supported and challenged by other followers of Christ. Wouldn't it be great to hang out in an environment with little selfishness or harmful comments? Imagine standing shoulder to shoulder with people of like mind and faith praising God and serving Him and others." [2]

Can you see it?

PART I
ENVISION ... THE LIFE

ENVISION: As a follower of Jesus the life you have is not just the mere existence of a living creature. You possess an *eternal* kind of life. To you this eternal life is more than just a *quantity* of life (lasting forever); it is a *quality* of life (going deeper). You have more than just a new religious orientation to life; you have a totally new life. You are not just a citizen of an earthly nation; you are a citizen in the Kingdom of God. You are not just on a quest to become a more moral person; there is something powerfully new inside of you that is pushing out into your exterior life. The good things that you do are not a tribute to your goodness, but to the goodness of the One, Jesus Christ, living in you. Your entire life is lived out of the reality of your new identity in Jesus Christ. Your sins ... past, present and future ... have all been covered by the blood of Jesus Christ. Your occasional sinful acts are the residual symptoms of a disease known as sin, from which you have been delivered, but with which you continue to struggle.

SCRIPTURAL FOUNDATION: Galatians 2:20; John 15:1-5; John 17:3; Matthew 28:18-20; Acts 2:41-47; Ephesians 2:8-10; 4:11-13; Colossians 1:28-29

PART I ~ DAY 1
THE GOSPEL OF DISCIPLESHIP

Today's Scripture Reading: Romans 1:11-17

The vision God had for us when, in His kind providence, He sent His Son to be our Savior is the essence of the gospel. We are not saved through the message of the gospel and then left to our own strength to do the best we can. No, the gospel is at the heart of what God envisions when we're first saved and when we reach heaven's shores ... and everything in between.

"Gospel" is a biblical and theological word that simply means "good news." It is an announcement of something that is true. It is nothing less than full acceptance of this gospel through faith and repentance that ushers a person into the eternal kind of life God envisions for us. This is why the Apostle Paul would confidently exclaim: "I am not ashamed of the gospel, because it is the power of God for the salvation of everyone who believes: first for the Jew, then for the Gentile. For in the gospel a righteousness from God is revealed, a righteousness that is by faith from first to last, just as it is written: 'The righteous will live by faith'" (Romans 1:16-17).

The gospel is the good news that Jesus Christ came to this earth, suffered and died in order to pay the penalty for our sin so that we may freely receive forgiveness and the gift of His righteousness. It is out of this gift of righteousness that the life of a Christ-follower is lived.

I live in Fort Worth, Texas, home to the famed Colonial Country Club and the Colonial Invitational Golf Tournament. Shortly after I moved to Fort Worth I heard the story told by a member of the club who took a guest there for lunch one day. His guest, having never been to the Colonial Country Club before, failed to wear a sport coat, which was mandatory for dining in that particular part of the club. The manager of the club said to the member, "I'm sorry, but your guest cannot enter the dining room without a sport coat."

The member pulled the manager aside and said, "Can you help us out here?" The manager said, "I'll see what I can do." The manager came back moments later with a sport coat, handed it to the guest and said, "You can wear this." The guest took a look at the loaner coat and was a bit reluctant to put it on. It was a red and green checkered sport coat! But he knew he had to wear it if he would be able to enter the member's dining room with his host. So the two men were seated for lunch. During their lunch fellow diners could be seen glancing over at the guest, who was wearing this brightly colored sport coat.

After lunch as they were leaving they returned the

coat to the manager. The manager said, "I guess you wondered why people were looking at you while you were eating lunch." The guest said, "Yes, as a matter of fact I was wondering. I felt quite uncomfortable." The manager continued, "The red and green checkered coat you were wearing is the sport coat given as a prize to the champion of the Colonial Invitational Tournament. I borrowed it from his locker."

Entrance into the Kingdom of God requires one be clothed in righteousness. Jesus taught: "For I tell you that unless your righteousness surpasses that of the Pharisees and the teachers of the law, you will certainly not enter the kingdom of heaven" (Matthew 5:20). That made entrance into God's Kingdom pretty much impossible for the average person who could not match the so-called righteousness of these religious professionals.

Jesus, however, was talking about a righteousness that was *not* attained by human performance. The righteousness required for entrance into His Kingdom must be granted by Jesus Himself. The Apostle Paul expressed his strong desire "(to) and be found in him (Christ), not having a righteousness of my own that comes from the law, but that which is through faith in Christ—the righteousness that comes from God and is by faith" (Philippians 3:9).

We must place our faith in the righteousness of Christ who died as a substitute for our sin on Calvary's cross. We must accept the provision He has made for our salvation. So when we stand before God to enter heaven we will be checked by the Father Himself to see if we are in proper attire ... wearing the righteous coat of the champion Jesus.

The gospel insures that the Christian life is for the glory of God from start to finish. "Seeing discipleship through the lens of the gospel means applying the gospel to all of life, believing transformation occurs when disciples center their lives on the gospel ... (The gospel) is not merely the foundational curriculum for a disciple but the overarching curriculum." [3]

Connecting discipleship and spiritual formation with the gospel is essential. All that God envisions for us is intended for His glory alone. The life lived by a disciple of Jesus is intended to bring glory to God (see Matthew 5:16). The gospel is vital to our *salvation*; it is also vital to our *sanctification*. When it comes to the Christian life we *start* with the gospel and then we *stand* in the gospel. To the believers in Corinth the Apostle Paul said, "Now, brothers, I want to remind you of the gospel I preached to you, which you received and on which you have taken your stand" (1 Corinthians 15:1). Notice that the gospel was "preached to" and "received" by those in the ancient city of Corinth. We are well familiar with this idea. It is what most of us understand about the gospel. It was preached to us; we received it and were saved. Notice, however, it didn't end there. Having been saved they now are to go on through life standing in the great truth that ongoing transformation still only happens through dependence upon and obedience to Christ.

All of this is summed up in the words of the contemporary hymn "In Christ Alone."

In Christ alone my hope is found
He is my light, my strength, my song
This Cornerstone, this solid ground
Firm through the fiercest drought and storm
What heights of love, what depths of peace
When fears are stilled, when strivings cease
My Comforter, my All in All
Here in the love of Christ I stand

In Christ alone, who took on flesh
Fullness of God in helpless babe
This gift of love and righteousness
Scorned by the ones He came to save
'Til on that cross as Jesus died
The wrath of God was satisfied
For every sin on Him was laid
Here in the death of Christ I live

There in the ground His body lay
Light of the world by darkness slain

Then bursting forth in glorious Day
Up from the grave He rose again
And as He stands in victory
Sin's curse has lost its grip on me
For I am His and He is mine
Bought with the precious blood of Christ

No guilt of life, no fear in death
This is the power of Christ in me
From life's first cry to final breath
Jesus commands my destiny
No power of hell, no scheme of man
Can ever pluck me from His hand
'til He returns or calls me home
Here in the power of Christ I'll stand.[4]

Take Away for Today: In the quest to grow in your knowledge of and likeness to Christ, you do not start with the gospel and then move on to something better or different. Stand today and every day in the salvation you have in Christ alone.

PART I ~ DAY 2
FOLLOW ME!

Today's Scripture Reading: Matthew 16:21-28

I would venture to say that most of us, when we had the gospel explained to us before we were saved, were not told that we were signing on for a life of following Jesus. What exactly did Jesus have in mind when He took our sins upon Himself as He died on the cross? It is that we would follow Him into a new life. When Christ called others to eternal life He said, "Deny yourself, take up your cross and follow me."

"To Christ's disciples, discipleship meant making a serious commitment to follow a leader." [5] Was this your understanding when you entered into your relationship with Christ? Was it made clear to you that coming to Christ and putting your trust in Him was not just an *agreement* you were making with Christ? It was a *commitment* you were making to Him. The experience of becoming a Christian is essentially trusting Jesus Christ enough to follow Him.

We must face the reality that most Christians do not see themselves as disciples, as followers of Jesus. Do you realize that the word "Christian" is used only 3 times in the New Testament? It was actually a derisive term originally given to believers by their enemies … "little Christs." Later, believers gladly embraced the name. The word "believer" is used about 27 times. The word "disciple" is used nearly 300 times. This is the way the Holy Spirit prefers to identify people who have put their faith in Christ.

A "disciple," simply put, is a learner, a student, an apprentice, a follower. The word "disciple" first appears in the gospels of Jesus' life and ministry where His followers were called disciples. However, the followers of Jesus were not the first to be called disciples. In the ancient Jewish culture in which Jesus appeared teachers called "rabbis" attracted students called "disciples." These disciples literally followed their Jewish teachers, who would often be seen walking as their students followed them, hanging on every word. Jesus' followers and others sometimes called Him "Rabbi." However, a careful study of the life and ministry of Jesus reveals that His relationship with His followers was more than just one of imparting knowledge. He literally transformed their lives as they followed Him.

The full picture of discipleship is seen in Dallas Willard's definition of a disciple as someone who has come into such a union, such a relationship, with Christ that they routinely do what Jesus taught. [6] Though we start our life as a believer with that purpose, it is a lifelong journey of that purpose becoming practice in our lives each day. So the vision God has for those of us who follow after Christ is that the interior life of His Son would be reproduced in us so that...

- We might depend on the Father as Jesus did
- We might worship the Father as Jesus did
- We might see other people the way Jesus did
- We might deal with temptation the way Jesus did
- We might cling to God's Word as Jesus did
- We might humble ourselves as Jesus did
- We might handle suffering as Jesus did

When I was a college student I was introduced to Walter Henrichsen's book *Disciples Are Made Not Born*.[7] The very title is a prophetic statement. After all, our Lord's "Great Commission" says this: "All authority in heaven and on earth has been given to me. Therefore go and *make disciples* of all nations, baptizing them in the name of the Father and of the Son and of the Holy Spirit, and teaching them to obey everything I have commanded you. And surely I am with you always, to the very end of the age" (Matthew 28:18-20, italics mine). So it is the task and challenge of every authentic New Testament church to remain vigorously focused on developing passionate followers of Christ.

Christian pollster George Barna describes this amazing journey: "Discipleship is becoming a complete and competent follower of Jesus Christ. It is about intentional training of people who voluntarily submit to the lordship of Christ and who want to become imitators of Him in every thought, word, and deed. On the basis of teaching, training, experiences, relationships and accountability, a disciple becomes transformed into the likeness of Jesus Christ. Discipleship, in other words, is about being and reproducing spiritually mature zealots for Christ." [8]

However, we have this dilemma in the church: Many church members do not see themselves as disciples. They think that one can be a Christian forever and never become a disciple. A typical Christian today thinks disciples are people who sit in the first-class section of the Christian life, and the rest sit back in the coach section. It doesn't matter where you sit because we're all going to the same destination.

For years this was true in my own experience. When I was saved as a teenager I had a mistaken, or at least an incomplete, view of what the gospel meant and what Christ wanted to do with my life. I wanted Him to forgive my sin and reserve a place in heaven for me, but Jesus had so much more in mind for me. He was calling me to follow Him, to walk with Him into a new life.

Some may say, "Well, this wasn't explained to me when I was saved. This isn't what I signed on for." Others may say, "Well, that's all fine and good for some believers, but I'm on a different plan." Someone has observed that this kind of Christian is just "auditing" Jesus, like they're just attending His "class" but are really not responsible to learn, change and grow.

So the challenge for the church is to raise the standard for what we expect for and from each other. The command of Jesus was to go and "make disciples" (Matthew 28:19). Our presenting of the gospel is to include the vision that those who are saved are becoming Christ-followers.

Somehow we have to impress upon people that this is a radical and serious calling, not just for a few believers, but for everyone who claims to be saved. Jesus unwaveringly called His disciples on these terms: "If anyone would come after me, he must deny himself and take up his cross and follow me. For whoever wants to save his life will lose it, but whoever loses his life for me will find it" (Matthew 16:24-25). When we make that choice, Jesus makes the change. We can look forward with great anticipation to the ways Christ will transform our lives.

Take Away for Today: Every act of your obedience to Christ today holds the promise of future transformation in your life as you follow Christ. As you go through this day try to imagine you are walking around with the invisible Christ, whom you are following as your Master.

PART I ~ DAY 3
THE PROGRESS PROCESS

Today's Scripture Reading: II Thessalonians 2:13-17

So often we think about the Christian life like a game of Monopoly. We keep moving around the board, going over the same spaces. After a while all the property is bought up, someone goes out of business and there is a winner. I prefer to think about growth in the Christian life in different terms. When you cut down a tree, you see the rings inside the tree trunk. Each ring represents a "season" of life and of growth. Each season of life builds upon the other.

Brad Waggoner perceptively describes the progress process in this way: "Salvation is not just a past-tense event and a future-tense reward; it is a present-tense journey that takes us from one end of life's rugged, narrow path to the other." [9]

To use another image, God, like a master sculptor, is doing a shaping work in us until the day we die. Years ago my wife and I were given a sculpture of David done by the late artist Walt Horton. Actually it is just a part of a much larger work of art that shows David after he slew the giant Goliath. David is standing with his foot on the massive head of Goliath. Nan and I, along with some other friends, had the privilege of being in Walt Horton's studio outside of Vail, Colorado a few years ago when this piece was still being sculpted from a rough piece of clay. In fact, the artist let us participate in the sculpting. He had done extensive study on David and his fight with Goliath. He asked us what we thought about the kind of expression David would have had after being victorious in the contest with Goliath. We discussed it and gave Walt our impressions and, as we spoke, he actually changed the expression on David's face. In the process, he removed any bits of clay that concealed the image the artist had in mind for the finished work.

That is what happens in spiritual formation. "For we are God's workmanship, created in Christ Jesus to do good works, which God prepared in advance for us to do" (Ephesians 2:10). Fittingly, the word for "workmanship" might also be translated "a work of art."

As we think about the seven attributes of a disciple, it is imperative that we not consider that these are things we do in our own strength apart from the message of the gospel. The grace of God that saved us is the grace of God that enables us to demonstrate the attributes of a follower of Jesus. The gospel establishes that all glory belongs to God in everything related to the Christian life. The life God envisioned for us He imparted to us through His Son Jesus Christ. Nothing we do in that grand quest should be done in our own strength, or as a means of somehow making God more pleased with us.

Thus, the learning and applying of the Word of God becomes the means by which we hear the word of Christ and are nourished in our faith. Obeying God and denying self are the means by which we demonstrate our love to Jesus who has graciously saved us. Serving God and others is the means by which we pour out our gratitude to God and His tender mercies toward others. Sharing Jesus Christ with others is the natural outgrowth of our relationship to the One who called His first disciples by saying, "Follow me and I will make you fishers of men" (Matthew 4:19). Living by faith means that we are continually sustained by God in all areas of life. When we seek God in worship we do so to glorify Him. Building Christ-centered relationships is for the purpose of living out a love that first existed in the Trinity, and that now has been imparted to us in Christ.

The biblical term for this process is "sanctification," which is different from justification. Bill Hull explains: "Justification is the new creation of the new person, and sanctification is the preservation, protection, and the development of that person until the day of Jesus Christ ... The act of faith that justifies is also the engine of sanctification; both are unified in discipleship, the lifelong journey of following and obeying Jesus." [10] Hull goes on to say: "Many Christians think the gospel was absolutely essential for justification (declared righteous by Christ) but has little to do with sanctification (the process of becoming more holy)." [11]

Consider how the Apostle Paul describes the progress process: "But we ought always to thank God for you, brothers loved by the Lord, because from the beginning God chose you to be saved through the sanctifying work of the Spirit and through belief in the truth. He called you to this through our gospel, that you might share in the glory of our Lord Jesus Christ" (2 Thessalonians 2:13-14).

Do you see it? From the very beginning of time God envisioned something magnificent happening in and to you. God chose you to be saved "through the sanctifying work of the Spirit." That is, God's shaping you into the likeness of His Son happens through the work of the Holy Spirit increasingly making you more and more sanctified or set apart of God's purposes.

There are two kinds of righteousness: positional righteousness and practical righteousness. Both are gifts of God's grace. *Positional righteousness* is imparted to us in our initial salvation as a gift of God's grace through faith. "(That I may) be found in him, not having a righteousness of my own that comes from the law, but that which is through faith in Christ—the righteousness that comes from God and is by faith" (Philippians 3:9).

Practical righteousness involves a process of growth in Christlikeness in the life God has for us. "You were taught, with regard to your former way of life, to put off your old self, which is being corrupted by its deceitful desires; to be made new in the attitude of your minds; and to put on the new self, created to be like God in true righteousness and holiness" (Ephesians 4:22-24).

On the eve of Jesus' crucifixion He spent vital moments with his closest friends and followers. Scholars believe that Jesus was walking through a vineyard on the way to the Mount of Olives when He stopped and pointed out the process of a healthy vine producing abundant fruit. "I am the vine; you are the branches. If a man remains in me and I in him, he will bear much fruit; apart from me you can do nothing" (John 15:5). The health of the vine was essential for the necessary end-product of fruit to appear. Pruning and careful tending of the vine would insure the production, not just of fruit, but of *much* fruit.

Herein Jesus describes the process by which His followers would grow and bear fruit. They would remain continuously connected to Jesus through abiding in and obedience to His Word. Practically speaking this is a deliberate effort to live each day exposed to the light and life of Jesus' words (and the entire Bible). The life of Christ is impossible to live apart from this vital union with Christ. It is as impossible as maintaining one's life underwater without the help of some source of oxygen.

The Father's purpose is the production of the fruit of Christ-likeness. This would only be possible as the life that exists in the vine flows out through the little branches (us) upon which would be borne the fruit of transformed lives.

For years I have been burdened that the church has sprinted past what was the main thing for Jesus – the development of passionate followers. We are informed enough to know that people ought to believe and behave differently when they become Christ-followers; but we are vastly ignorant of the process by which that happens. We expect outward results (fruit), and often manufacture fake fruit, but we do not know the supernatural process by which real spiritual fruit is actually produced. "But the fruit of the Spirit is love, joy, peace, patience, kindness, goodness, faithfulness, gentleness, self-control; against such things there is no law" (Galatians 5:22-23).

Just stop to examine those words carefully. As you do, you may come to realize that there is only one person in all of history who has ever completely fleshed out those virtues. The "fruit of the Spirit" is the very life of Christ. If you want to know what this life is that God envisions for us you simply look at Jesus. It's all about Him.

Take Away for Today: The reason God has not taken you on to heaven is that there is a process of sanctification (spiritual formation) that is taking place in your life this very day. Eagerly watch for how God is working.

PART 1 ~ DAY 4
FOLLOWING JESUS INTO LIFE

Today's Scripture Reading: Luke 9:18-27

As Jesus approached His crucifixion He explained to His disciples what it meant for Him. He said, "The Son of Man must suffer many things and be rejected by the elders, chief priests and teachers of the law, and he must be killed and on the third day be raised to life" (Luke 9:22). Jesus' followers must know that this would have implications for them as well: "If anyone would come after me, he must deny himself and take up his cross daily and follow me" (Luke 9:23).

The meaning of Jesus' words must have been staggering to His disciples: "I am going down a road that will be marked with unbelievable suffering on my part, but that will result in unimaginable life for you. But if you are going to get that life, you're going to have to go down the same road that I am going down. For Me, going down this road will mean literal death; but on the other side My Father will raise Me up. For you, going down this road will mean death of another kind … death to your old way of life, death to your own personal right to rule your destiny ... death to self. But on the other side of that decision you make to go down that road, My Father will perform the same miracle. He will raise you up to walk in a new life ... and one day even to a resurrection of your body to something unimaginably glorious."

There's more to the cross of Christ than most of us realize. I'm talking about the grand doctrine of the cross of Jesus Christ – not just the historical fact that Jesus Christ died on a Roman cross – not just *what* He did, but *why* He did it. Did Jesus endure so much agony to provide forgiveness for sins? Absolutely yes! To provide a way for sinners to go to heaven when they die? Most certainly, but there's more! As Jesus died on the cross He envisioned for us a way of life that explodes with the power of God.

That's why Paul would say, "I want to know Christ and the power of his resurrection and the fellowship of sharing in his sufferings, becoming like him in his death, and so, somehow, to attain to the resurrection from the dead" (Philippians 3:10-11).

Now look carefully at the amazing invitation Jesus extends: "Then he said to them all: 'If anyone would come after me, he must deny himself and take up his cross daily and follow me'" (Luke 9:23). Jesus' words cut through the commonly held, contemporary definitions of what it means to be a "Christian." Look at how Jesus lays it out:

First, there is a choice to be made. He said "*if* anyone would come after me..." Jesus gave listeners a clear choice to move out of one group of people into another group of people.

Notice that Jesus "said to them all…" To whom is Jesus speaking? A few verses earlier Luke writes that while Jesus was praying in private with His disciples He asked them, "Who do the crowds say I am?" (Luke 9:18). There are two groups Jesus identifies here … the disciples and the crowds. When you read the gospels you see that around Jesus there were hundreds, sometimes thousands of people who were part of the crowd of admirers. They heard Jesus' amazing teachings. They watched Him work miracles. They sensed that He really cared about them. They admired Him … but they did not follow Him. An admirer is awed; a follower is committed. An admirer applauds; a follower surrenders. An admirer approves; a follower obeys.

Next, Jesus describes the course to be taken. "If anyone would *come after me…*" The words "come after me" show us what it means to be a disciple of Jesus. Later Jesus said, "Anyone who does not carry his cross and follow me cannot be my disciple" (Luke 14:27).

As I mentioned earlier I was saved as a young teenager. The church where I started attending had a caring, Bible-preaching pastor, as well as a fun youth group. However, because I didn't really know how to walk with Christ, my life didn't change very much. I remember thinking I could now join the Fellowship of Christian Athletes at my school, because now I was one. Other than that there wasn't much different about me as far as my buddies could tell. It wasn't until I started college that I was introduced to some people who were living a life that was radically different ... people who followed Christ passionately ... who took seriously the teachings of Jesus Christ.

Remember Dallas Willard's definition of a disciple as someone who has come into such a union, such a relationship, with Christ that they routinely do what Jesus taught.

The key word there is *routinely*. I remember when I first began to take Christ seriously, I was really surprised when I got something right. Before I was a Christ-follower I didn't think much about the language that I used. After I was saved I remember catching myself just before that word slipped out and thinking, "Jesus said to let my 'yes' be yes and my 'no' be no. Don't swear." Over time those rare victories became a more consistent pattern in my life.

Research reveals that fewer people in the US now identify themselves as "Christians." Even with that, 78% of Americans still call themselves Christians. [12] What they probably mean is if they are going to pick a religion, the religion of Jesus would be a good one because they are familiar with what Jesus taught and did. But that's pretty much as far as it goes for them, except for those who cross that line and move to the level that Christ had in mind ... followers of Christ.

For many people who carry that label "Christian," their relationship to Jesus goes like this: I want to use Jesus to get into heaven when I die. I want to use Jesus to give me peace. I want to use Jesus to soothe my guilty conscience. I want to use Jesus to be there for me. The fact is that Jesus makes all of that available to us. The problem is, however, that we want all the perks Jesus offers without being willing to follow Him in the life He calls us to live.

That's why for many church-goers in America there is no real distinction between the way they live their lives Monday to Saturday and the lifestyle of person who makes no claim to be a Christian. Following Jesus means following Him into a transformed life.

Jesus did it then and He is doing it now. He is calling people out of the crowd to become His followers … His disciples … someone who has such a vital union with Christ that they routinely do what Jesus taught. He's calling people to step out of the crowd to become one of those extraordinary individuals.

One might hear this call of Jesus and wonder, "Is Christ just trying to make my life miserable?" No! He has in mind a life for us that is only possible when we follow Him into this kind of life. Jesus describes it this way: "For whoever wants to save his life will lose it, but whoever loses his life for me will save it. What good is it for a man to gain the whole world, and yet lose or forfeit his very self?" (Luke 9:24-25).

Take Away for Today: Is it possible or practical to expect Christians to really live this kind of radical life? Yes it is because that's exactly what Christ envisioned for you when you started the journey with Him.

PART I ~ DAY 5
DON'T MISS THE LIFE

Today's Scripture Reading: Matthew 19:16-26

We must not be distracted from pursuing the life that Jesus envisioned for His followers – from the life God envisioned for us when He sent His Son to die on the cross of Calvary. Did God have in mind the forgiveness of our sins? Certainly. Did God picture the end result of our being with Him in heaven for eternity? Absolutely, but that's not all He envisioned. God saw a *life* … a quality of life that is to be lived out every day on our way to heaven. Discipleship means choosing that life.

Consider Jesus' encounter with an affluent young man. He has been labeled through the ages as "the rich, young ruler." Three of the four gospel writers include this interchange in their accounts (Matthew 19; Mark 10; Luke 18); the Holy Spirit wanted to make sure we didn't miss this. The man approached Jesus with a question: "Teacher, what good thing must I do to get eternal life?" (Matthew 19:16). Jesus immediately sees the faulty approach to the question, but He presses on. "If you want to enter life, obey the commandments," (v.17b). Don't misunderstand this; Jesus is not prescribing a works-based way to eternal life. No, to the contrary, He is leading the man to an important realization. It's as if Jesus is saying, "Alright, let's follow this line of reasoning for a moment. You want to know what good thing you must *do* to get eternal life? Well, start with this." Then Jesus recounts six of the well-known commands: '"Do not murder, do not commit adultery, do not steal, do not give false testimony, honor your father and mother … love your neighbor as yourself" (Matthew 19:18b-19). The first five commands Jesus recites are from the Ten Commandments. The last one He mentions ("love your neighbor as yourself") is a general command from Leviticus 19:18 which summarizes the horizontal elements of the Ten Commandments related to how we treat others.

"So far, so good," the young man reasons. He honestly believes he has done a very acceptable job at keeping the righteous demands. "Check! What else?" And this is where Jesus has been leading the conversation all along. The Lord slams the door on the young man's attempt to earn eternal life through his own righteousness with the lofty demand: "If you want to be perfect, go, sell your possessions and give to the poor, and you will have treasure in heaven. Then come, follow me" (Matthew 19:21).

Jesus' statement blasted a huge hole in this young man's self-righteousness. In fact, the young man hadn't actually kept the Law. The point Jesus is making is that none of us can, in our own strength, completely adhere to the lofty demands of the Law of God. Only by trusting in the righteousness of Christ can anyone have eternal life. Jesus was calling the man to a life of trust and selfless abandonment in following Himself. Tragically, the Bible says the young man went away sad because he was very wealthy.

Jesus was not about to allow the young man to get away with something less than full and complete surrender to Himself, which is at the heart of saving faith. The life Jesus envisioned for this man, and for all of His followers, was a life that is so vitally connected to Christ that He governs every aspect of our lives. Jesus was after more than just another admirer or fan; He was about developing a passionate follower.

I have to admit that, as a pastor, I stand indicted at this point. I have been guilty of lowering the costly demands of following Jesus. If I had been dealing with this young man I would have found a way to let him off the hook. A good leader would never let a guy like this get away. This is the kind of person you can build your church on. With a church full of people like this you could "take the city," as we pastors are fond of saying. After all, he fits the profile perfectly. He's young. The measure of just about any church's vitality is, "Are the young people coming to your church." We chase cool because cool attracts youth.

The man was young and distinguished. The Gospel

of Luke comments that the man was a "ruler." The word described one who was in a prominent position. Again, any aggressive leader wants to go after other leaders. We may wonder, "How could Jesus let a guy like this get away? Imagine the good this prominent man could do for the image of Jesus' cause."

But there's more. This young ruler also happened to be rich, which was the sticking point in his encounter with Jesus. Jesus, however, was not the least bit impressed with the man's worldly riches. Jesus desired greater riches for the young man. Here again, pastors have fallen prey to the worldly model that cringes to see this kind of wealth walk away from Jesus. "Let's find some way to keep him onboard. Just think of the programs we can put on and the buildings we can put up with that kind of money." But Jesus would not cut the guy any slack. The life He envisioned for this man was far greater than his riches and position could offer.

Don't misunderstand. Jesus has nothing against the young, the prominent or the affluent. In fact, the Bible and church history reveal the gospel impacting countless numbers from each of these categories. But whomever Jesus calls to Himself ... young or old; rich or poor; well-known or unknown ... He simply will not allow them to settle for anything less than full surrender.

As you come to the end of this first section, perhaps you realize that you have never repented of your sin and placed your faith in Jesus Christ. A simple way to describe the biblical response of one who needs to be saved can be seen in the letters A-B-C.

- **A** – Admit that you are a sinner in need of God's life. "For all have sinned and fall short of the glory of God" (Romans 3:23).
  "For the wages of sin is death…" (Romans 6:23a).

- **B** – Believe (put your trust in) Christ to save you from your sin.
  "For God so loved the world that he gave his one and only Son, that whoever believes in him shall not perish but have eternal life" (John 3:16).

- **C** – Confess
  "That if you confess with your mouth, 'Jesus is Lord,' and believe in your heart that God raised him from the dead, you will be saved. For it is with your heart that you believe and are justified, and it is with your mouth that you confess and are saved" (Romans 10:9-10).

If you are genuinely ready to put your trust in Christ for this new life, you can say something like this to God in prayer: "Lord, I know I am a sinner, and my sins have separated me from you. I turn my back on my old way of life, and I turn to you in faith that you will give me eternal life. Thank you for loving me and for dying for my sins. I commit myself completely to you. In your Name I pray. Amen."

Take Away for Today: If you have made this life-changing commitment I encourage you to speak with a pastor, a church leader or another mature believer who can help you to begin your journey of following Christ into the life He envisions for you. Reading this book is a good place to start, but personally connecting with a more mature Christ-follower will help you to begin to grow.

PART II
ENVISION ... LEARNING
THE TRUTH OF GOD

ENVISION: You feast daily on God's Word, sincerely desiring to discover God's will for your life. It controls your thoughts, feelings and outlook. Your knowledge of the Father, Son and Holy Spirit increases as you immerse yourself in the Bible. You find yourself increasingly turning to the wisdom and truth of Scripture to guide the decisions you make each day. Your mind is being continuously renewed by the truths of Scripture. The Bible's great and precious promises support your life with strength, endurance, perseverance and patience. The Holy Spirit is making the Bible come alive for you as you read, study, memorize and meditate on Scripture. Each time you open your Bible you realize you are having an encounter with the Living God. You have a teachable spirit that immediately responds to truth that is taught and preached. You savor Christ revealed on every page of the Bible. You seek to apply Scriptural truth in behavior and decision-making, resulting in a Christ-like lifestyle.

SCRIPTURAL FOUNDATION: Joshua 1:8; Psalm 119; Matthew 28:18-20; Luke 11:28; John 8:31-32; Acts 2:41-42; II Timothy 3:14-17: James 1:22-25; II Peter 1:4-8; I John 2:5-6

PART II ~ DAY 1
THE CONDITION OF YOUR HEART

Today's Scripture Reading: Matthew 13:1-9, 18-23

Imagine what it must have been like before the universe was created. Nothing or no one existed but God alone. It's impossible for us to comprehend the vastness of our material universe. Just try to wrap your brain around the *absence* of this universe we inhabit. Then the Bible explains to us that all of that instantly and dramatically changed when "God said..." (Genesis 1:3). With a word God spoke the universe and its inhabitants into existence. God's Word is powerful!

The life God envisions for us is imparted through the Word of God. "For you have been born again, not of perishable seed, but of imperishable, through the living and enduring word of God" (1 Peter 1:23). One of the many names given to Jesus in the Scriptures is "the Word." Jesus is God's very Word spoken to us through the life He lived. We are saved after having heard the Word of God, the gospel. When we become Christ-followers we are new-born spiritual babies who need to be nourished by the food of God's Word. The guidance we need in the Christian life comes by the Word of God and the Spirit of God.

I cannot overstate how essential God's Word is to the life that God envisions for us in His Son Jesus Christ. So it is vitally important for us to learn how to properly receive the Word of the Lord.

Preparing our hearts to receive the seed of God's Word is much like preparing soil for plants. I'm not fond of gardening. I do it because my wife likes colorful things around the yard. I've suggested we go to Wal-Mart and pick up some artificial flowers and stick them in our flower beds. She frowns and rolls her eyes at that suggestion. Ain't gonna happen!

A few years ago Nan and I made our annual trek to a local nursery to pick out the plants we wanted to enjoy through the summer months. Typically my job is to get the plants in the ground, and keep them watered. The soil around our house is a dense mixture of rocks and clay. When the ground is wet it's like trying to handle Play-Doh … not the best conditions for plant growth. That is remedied by mixing in several bags of planting mix to break up the gooey consistency of the soil. Of course, this means hours of sore muscles and sweat … which is why I skipped that step on this particular year. Just stick the plants in the ground and water them good. There, that should do it.

Later in the season I was looking at our flower beds and it seemed that the plants hadn't really grown much. By that time each year the plants are usually well-developed and the beds are full of color. Not so this particular year. Some of the plants weren't much larger than when I planted them two months before. I reasoned, "Oh the nursery just gave us some wimpy plants. They can't stand the heat." Yeah right! I didn't want to admit it, but the problem is that I took shortcuts in preparing the soil for the plants. Their roots were having a hard time pushing through the Play-Doh they were planted in. They really didn't have a chance of reaching their lush, colorful potential.

The same thing happens to the human heart.

Jesus told a parable about a farmer who sowed some seed in his field (Matthew 13). Some of the seed fell on hard-packed ground; the seeds had no chance of taking root before the birds came and pecked away the seed. Some of the seed fell into shallow soil. Immediately the seed took root, but not deeply. When the hot sun began to bear down on the little plants they shriveled and died for lack of sufficient roots. Still other seed fell into a patch of soil that was already loaded with weeds and thorns. There was too much competition for the nutrients in the soil, and the plants simply didn't grow to produce fruit.

Later Jesus explained that the various soils in the parable represent the differing conditions of the human heart when it comes into contact with the seed of God's Word. For some people their hearts are so hard that they hardly know when a seed of truth has been dropped before them. For some there is initial interest in God's Word, but the shallowness of their heart simply won't sustain any consistent growth when hard times come. For others the Word of God falls into such a distracted heart that the Word cannot compete with all the other interests. Little, if any, fruit appears from this life. As Jesus puts it, "the worries of this life and the deceitfulness of wealth choke it, making it unfruitful" (Matthew 13:22)

Francis Chan in his book *Crazy Love* makes the following observation: "I think most American churchgoers are the soil that chokes the seed because of all the thorns. Thorns are anything that distracts us from God. When we want God and a bunch of other stuff, then that means we have thorns in our soil. A relationship with God simply cannot grow when money, sins, activities, favorite sports teams, addictions or commitments are piled on top of it." [13]

Our lives are simply too crowded to seriously seek God and the life of the gospel. No wonder we see little fruit in terms of genuine Christlikeness reflected in our lives. For this to change we must take an honest look at the multiple interests, hobbies, gadgets and amusements we have heaped upon our lives. What will have to go in order for us to have more time to devote to seeking the Kingdom of God and His righteousness? Hours in front of the television? Absorption with mindless entertainment? Endless interaction on social media? Infatuation with the latest fashions or cars?

I'm not calling for a monkish lifestyle. I'm not saying we should not take pleasure in the delightful experiences of life. God has given us all things to richly enjoy. I'm saying that we should passionately give ourselves to that which brings most glory to God. Our most aggressive pursuits should be after that which will produce eternal fruit ... hearts filled with love for God, minds shaped by life-changing truth, the gospel of Christ extended to the ends of the earth, souls brought into the Kingdom of God, and the glory of God over all things.

In His parable Jesus spoke about a fourth kind of soil. "Still other seed fell on good soil, where it produced a crop" (v.8). This is the heart, Jesus explains, that "hears the word and understands it" (v.23). Seed sown into hearts like this creates a harvest of a hundred, sixty or thirty times what was originally sown.

Take Away for Today: So what's the condition of your heart? Set your heart wholly on the knowledge of God. Love Him with *all* of your heart, soul, mind and strength. May that all-consuming passion crowd out the lesser priorities so that you may live a truly fruitful life.

PART II ~ DAY 2
THE PLAN

Today's Scripture Reading: Matthew 4:1-11

When Vince Lombardi became the new coach of the Green Bay Packers in 1959 the team had fallen to the bottom of the league standings. Player and fan morale was sagging. Lombardi faced a real challenge in turning the franchise around. Legend has it that at the beginning of that first season the famous coach gathered his team around him and uttered five words that have become some of the better known words in the field of motivation: "Gentlemen, this is a football." From there Lombardi took his team back through the basics of how a team goes about winning football games. Supposedly Lombardi began the first practice of every season with the same words: "Gentlemen, this is a football." During Vince Lombardi's tenure as head coach the Green Bay Packers rose to prominence, even dominance, in professional football. It was a tribute to his dogged determination to master the basics of the sport.

As we think about the life God envisions for us as followers of Jesus Christ there is nothing more basic to that life than the Word of God. It would be ridiculous to play the game of football without a football; and it's ridiculous to attempt to live the life of a Christ-follower without the Word of God.

I know of no one who is seriously following Christ whose life is not saturated in a regular, consistent way with the Word of God. "Gentlemen, this is a football." It's that foundational to the walk of the believer.

Perhaps the most basic discipline in the life of a disciple of Jesus is time alone with God each day. Jesus made this a practice, and followers of Jesus will do the same. The gospel writers tell us that "Jesus often withdrew to lonely places and prayed" (Luke 5:16).

We can only imagine how rich were the times of communion that Jesus enjoyed with His Father. What depths of intimacy did Jesus and the Father experience on those precious occasions? Of course Jesus lived in continuous fellowship with His Father. There was never a moment when Jesus was "offline," spiritually speaking.

Unfortunately, that is not the case for us. Struggling as we do with worldly or sinful distractions, we can easily let the days slip by without turning aside to enjoy time alone with God in the Word and in prayer.

Luke's account of the life and teachings of Jesus gives us some valuable insight into Jesus devotional relationship with His Father. We learn from Him how to have a successful devotional experience with the Lord.

"But Jesus often withdrew to lonely places and prayed" (Luke 5:16).

A PRIORITY

Notice that Jesus "withdrew." He understood how the distractions and interruptions of the daily life could crowd out the most important meeting He would ever have … His meeting with God. Success in this realm requires a determination to turn aside from the things that normally consume our attention so we can focus on the Lord and His Word. If Jesus, the eternal Son of God, needed time alone with the Father, how dare we think that we can get by without it?

For many of us our day revolves around the intake of physical food. Most of us head straight for the breakfast table when we awaken each day. Before long we're thinking about where and when we will eat lunch. Most wives and mothers know that the first thing they hear as the family returns home from work or school is, "Mom, what's for dinner?" What if we placed the same priority on the intake of the spiritual food of God's Word.

A PERIOD

Jesus would "often" slip away for time alone with the Father. This was no sporadic activity. We read on numerous occasions in the New Testament when Jesus went off to spend time with God. In the Sermon on the Mount our Savior gave careful instructions to His disciples about time alone with the Father in prayer. I cannot imagine Jesus teaching His disciples to do something He didn't do habitually.

In order to be consistent in our time alone with God we should have a set time that we routinely meet Him. For many, the best time is in the mornings. Granted, to do this means one having to get out of bed earlier than usual, or spending less time reading the morning paper, or checking in on social media. If you have an early flight to catch at the airport, you set your alarm to get up early so you won't miss the flight. Isn't time with God more important? Others prefer a different time for their devotions. The important thing is to make it a habit.

This may be particularly challenging for mothers with small children. Creativity and commitment will help you to find time to meet God on a regular basis.

A PLACE

Jesus withdrew to "lonely places" for this essential time alone with God. The word translated "lonely places" means deserted, uninhabited places. Jesus knew that He needed at times to be away from other people so He could focus His heart and mind on His heavenly Father. To do this meant finding a place where He would not be disturbed by others.

To go along with the habit of meeting God at a set time, it is also good to have a set place. Find a quiet place in your house where you can keep your Bible, prayer list and other devotional resources. Imagine God sitting in the chair next to you as you spend time with Him. In time that place will become "holy ground" for you.

A PLAN

Luke 5:16 says that Jesus sought time alone with the Father in order to pray. Jesus, limited as He was in the human body and experience, vitally depended on His Father for strength. Jesus accessed this strength in prayer. We also know that Jesus had the Scriptures memorized. After all, Jesus was and is the Word of God. His recorded prayers in the gospels show that Jesus prayed out of His knowledge of Scripture. When He was alone praying in the Wilderness of Temptation (Matthew 4) Jesus answered each of Satan's temptations with Scripture that He knew from memory. Jesus was daily immersed in the truth of God's Word.

The two most important components to a successful devotional life are the Word of God and prayer. Have a systematic plan for reading Scripture, whether it is in small or large portions. Many Bible reading plans are available in print and online. Often some kind of devotional book can help to focus our thinking on the Word of God. After a time of reading, studying and meditating on Scripture, our faith should be sufficiently recharged for us to enter into fervent prayer. While much of our praying will be spontaneous, Spirit-led conversation with the Father, it is also helpful to have a systematic plan for our praying. An ongoing prayer list is essential. The list might include people and things that we pray about daily or weekly. A prayer list strengthens our faith as we are able to note when the prayers have been answered.

I have found that a journal is an indispensable part of an effective devotional life. In my journal I record insights God gives me from Scripture, prayer needs and answers to prayer. The practice of devotional writing and journaling seems to reinforce what the Lord is doing and saying in my life. At the end of each year I enjoy reading back through my journal and being reminded of the faithfulness of God in the past year.

In my own personal devotional life I often use a devotional aide, like the book you are reading. These resources should not be the main course of our spiritual meal, but a side dish to add to our experience with God each day.

The important thing is to have a plan. If you don't you will find yourself struggling each day to fit in one of the most important components of any day for a believer … time alone with God. A plan will keep you moving forward through the year. It's like a consistent exercise program; you will find yourself in better spiritual condition week by week.

No doubt there will be times when your devotional

routine is interrupted. Don't be legalistic about this. If you miss a day, or even a week, just pick up where you left off and keep going. Don't give in to the condemnation of the enemy. If you forget or get too busy to eat a meal, you don't quit eating altogether. You're even hungrier for the next meal. The same thing holds true for your time alone with God in His Word.

Take Away for Today: No appointment we have each day is more important that our appointment with God when we come into His presence, feed on His Word, and pour out our hearts to Him in prayer. Make it a priority.

PART II ~ DAY 3
THE PROFITABLE WORD

Today's Scripture Reading: Psalm 119:1-16

What did we ever do without GPS? Hard-copy maps are virtually a thing of the past now that we have smart phones and built-in guidance systems in our cars. Sophisticated software now guides us turn-by-turn to our destination. Now it is commonly known that males are typically resistant to asking for directions. There's a chromosome missing in us that keeps us from admitting that we don't know which way to go. However, we do have an extra chromosome when it comes to all things tech. The prospect of another gadget sets our hearts racing with anticipation. So maybe the new GPS gadgets will keep those of us of the male gender on course.

The greatest need we have for direction in life is to know the way we are to live. God's Word provides a spiritual GPS system for us. Think of it as *God's* Positioning System rather than Global Positioning System.

The Bible has an incredible amount to say about itself, but none is more pointed and powerful than in Paul's letter to his young preacher friend Timothy: "All Scripture is God-breathed and is useful for teaching, rebuking, correcting and training in righteousness, so that the man of God may be thoroughly equipped for every good work" (2 Timothy 3:16-17).

Think for a moment about what these two short verses tell us about the Word of God. First we see the Bible is *reliable*. All Scripture is God-breathed. In other words, it is the very breath of God. When you speak others are able to hear you because breath (air) from inside your body (your lungs) moves across your vocal chords causing a distinct sound or word. So when you speak a word it is literally breathed by you. The same thing is true with God. The words of Scripture are literally breathed out by God. We believe that God is perfect in every way. He is the very essence of truth. So nothing coming from God can be imperfect or untruthful. So is our confidence in the reliability of Scripture. The Bible claims this for itself: "Above all, you must understand that no prophecy of Scripture came about by the prophet's own interpretation. For prophecy never had its origin in the will of man, but men spoke from God as they were carried along by the Holy Spirit" (2 Peter 1:20-21).

The Bible is a supernatural, miraculous book. I like to encourage people to think of this in terms of a string of numbers: 1400/66/44/1. The Bible was written over a span of about 1400 years. It contains 66 different books written by approximately 44 authors. The Bible, however, conveys 1 unique story. Isn't it amazing that the Bible was written over such a broad timeframe by so many different authors, yet when those sixty-six books are finally put together, in some instance hundreds of years after they were written, there is a single story woven throughout? This all points to the fact that, while God used humans in bringing the Bible into existence, it is not a human book. The Bible is divine and, as such, it is reliable.

II Timothy 3:16-17 not only tells us the Bible is *reliable*, but also that it is *profitable* or *useful.* It is useful in at least four different ways:

First, it is useful for *teaching.* Going back to the analogy of GPS, the Bible shows us the way we are to go in the journey of life. It teaches us the way we are to live our lives. It reveals to us the values of God and the proper way we are to think and act. We read God's Word for the purpose of knowing these vital truths that form the foundation for our life.

Teaching is one of the main components of the mission Christ has given to the church. The Great Commission of our Lord found in Matthew 28:18-20 instructs the church to make disciples, "teaching them to obey everything I have commanded you" (v.20). When the church gathers we should have a regular feast of the teaching of the precious truths of God's Word. One of the reasons we should not forsake the gathering of the church is that during those times we are encouraged and edified (Hebrews 10:25). This encouragement and edification comes primarily through the faithful teaching of God's Word.

Second, the Bible is useful for *rebuking*. Occasionally all of us get off of the path of God's way. The essence of sin is going our way rather than God's way. When that happens, God has provided His Word to show us when we get off the right way. To rebuke someone is to point out where they have gone wrong. As we read God's Word we may expect that the Spirit of God will use the Word of God to show us how we have sinned. Thankfully that's not where the ministry of the Word ends.

Third, the Bible is useful for *correcting*. Aren't you grateful that God doesn't just point out the bad things we have done. He loves us with a redeeming love and wants the very best for us. So God in His Word corrects us by showing us the way to make things right. You may have grown up with abusive parents who were quick to rebuke, but never loving enough to correct … to show you how to get back on the right path. Proper and loving discipline always includes rebuke and correction. God never rebukes us without also showing us the way to make it right.

Fourth, the Bible is useful for *training*. God is good to show us the right way to go (teaching), and to show us when we have gotten off the right way (rebuking), and to show us how to get back on the right way (correcting). But wouldn't it be great if we could be so trained and conditioned that we simply stayed on the right way continuously. Here, again, is where God's Word is so useful to us. As we continually fill our minds with the truths of Scripture we are training ourselves to repeat godly behavior. In a later chapter we will talk about the various spiritual "workouts" (also known as "disciplines") that help us to grow spiritually. Many of them involve the Word of God.

Whenever we engage God's Word we are engaging Christ, even if we happen to be reading or studying some portion of the Bible other than the gospels. This happened for two disciples of Jesus shortly after His resurrection. The account, given to us in Luke 24, reveals the two disciples are discouraged as they returned from Jerusalem to their home in Emmaus. They were discouraged because, so far as they knew, the One in whom they had put their hopes had been crucified by the Roman authorities. As they walked along they rehashed the horrible chain of events that resulted in Jesus of Nazareth being cruelly slain upon a Roman cross of crucifixion. Suddenly a Stranger appears on the road and walks with them. He inquires as to the things the two had been discussing. They were amazed that this traveler was apparently not familiar with all that had occurred, but they explained it all to Him. They had "hoped that he (Jesus) was the one who was going to redeem Israel" (Luke 24:21). Some women had gone to the tomb earlier that day and found that it was empty. There was even some speculation that Jesus was actually alive, but they could not verify that.

They are surprised when the Stranger rebuked them: "He said to them, 'How foolish you are, and how slow of heart to believe all that the prophets have spoken! Did not the Christ have to suffer these things and then enter his glory?' And beginning with Moses and all the Prophets, he explained to them what was said in all the Scriptures concerning himself" (Luke 24:25-27).

It was only after the disciples invited their unidentified travelling companion to join them for a meal that Jesus revealed His identity to them. After Jesus went on His way, "They asked each other, 'Were not our hearts burning within us while he talked with us on the road and opened the Scriptures to us?'" (Luke 24:32).

Your study of God's Word will explode with new life when you realize that you are encountering Christ on every page of your Bible. Remember that Jesus showed these early disciples how Moses and all the Prophets spoke of Him. Later they were amazed how their hearts burned within them as Jesus opened the Scriptures to them. That's what happens when you and I walk with Jesus. Jesus, through the ministry of the Holy Spirit, opens our eyes to see the full picture of all that God has done for us in Christ. When we read and study the Bible through this lens we come to understand the gospel and the life God has for us in His Son, Jesus Christ.

Take Away for Today: The life God envisioned for you when He sent His Son to die for your sins and to be raised from the dead is clearly spelled out in His Word. Whether you realize it or not, every time you open your Bible you are having an encounter with God.

PART II ~ DAY 4
GETTING A WORD FROM GOD

Today's Scripture Reading: Psalm 119:17-32

The purpose of our time in God's word is not just for *information*. Certainly the information we gain is truth and wisdom from on high. The main goal, however, of Bible study is *transformation*. For Bible study to transform us it has to become practical for us. Of course, we don't have to *make* the Bible practical. It *is* practical. God will speak to you in His Word about Himself and about your life. In fact, every time you open your Bible to read or study, you are having an encounter with God, whether you realize it or not.

As a pastor I've discovered that many believers have a hard time allowing God to speak to them through His Word. I believe we all want to come away from an encounter in personal Bible study and feel that we have heard from God. The Psalmist knew this when he prayed: "Fulfill your promise to your servant, so that you may be feared" (Psalm 119:38). There was a time when God spoke to the Psalmist. Was it from God's written word or through some other means? We are not told. We simply know that on that occasion God personally spoke a promise to His servant.

Certainly the primary way that God speaks to all people today is through His written word, the Bible. Yet there are times when we know that God has spoken *personally* to us through His Word. There was a time many years ago when my wife and I were faced with one of the most important decisions of our lives. There were many complicating factors that made God's will difficult to discern. Obviously we knew we needed to intensely seek God. We prayed earnestly; we read God's word with great vigilance believing that God gives guidance in the course of our regular reading of Scripture. It was during that period that the promise of Proverbs 3:5-6 became genuinely real to us: "Trust in the Lord with all your heart and lean not on your own understanding; in all your ways acknowledge him, and he will make your paths straight." We had read those verses many times before, but by the Holy Spirit's leading, we were convinced that God brought those verses to our attention to guide us through the decision-making process. It was a "word" from God. We were able to set aside our compulsion to "figure out" the right way to go. We simply put our whole-hearted trust in the Lord and continued to acknowledge (look to) Him, believing that He would direct our path. Of course, He did. When the time came we were able to make our decision with the confidence that God had shown us His will.

We must exercise great caution when we are seeking a word from God for our situation. We may easily take a verse out of context, claiming something that God never intends to give us. I remember the humorous story of a man who was discouraged. Wanting guidance from his Bible the man decided to just blindly open his Bible, put his finger on a verse and see what it said. His finger landed on Matthew 27:5 that says that Judas "went away and hanged himself." The discouraged man thought, "Oh know. Surely that is not what God is telling me to do." So he decided to try again. Blindly opening his Bible he put his finger on another page. This time his finger rested on Luke 10:37 that says, "You go, and do likewise." The man is severely shaken. "This can't be right," he reasoned. Hoping for different light he tried the procedure again. This time his finger landed on John 13:27 which reads, "What you are about to do, do quickly." That silly story is a classic illustration of how taking verses out of context can be dangerous.

So how do we open our Bibles needing a word from the Lord, but avoiding the hazards of faulty interpretation? Years ago I learned a simple approach to feeding on God's Word so that I am most likely to hear what the Holy Spirit is saying to me from that text. This approach involves a few very strategic steps:

Step #1 – Prepare. As you begin your study time, ask God to open your mind and heart to the things He wants to say to you through the text you are studying. We all know how easy it is for us to read over words but not really see what God is saying through them. Again, remember that as you approach the reading and study of your Bible, you are approaching God. The Bible says that the pure in heart will "see God" (Matthew 5:8).

Step #2 – Proximity. Read the passage, including the paragraphs before and after. It may even be necessary to read the preceding and succeeding chapters around the text you are studying. The purpose of this step is to see the *text* in its proper *context.* The verses in proximity to your text most often contain the key to unlocking the proper understanding of the passage you are studying. Again, taking Bible verses out of their context can lead to a faulty interpretation and to wrong decisions.

Step #3 – Paraphrase. This step involves writing a two- or three-sentence summary of the passage in your own words. Restating what the passage is actually saying moves you a step closer to understanding the truth of God revealed in the text. Certain passages of Scripture may seem confusing and difficult to understand. Don't be discouraged at this. The Bible says that God's ways are not our ways, and His thoughts are not our thoughts (Isaiah 55:9). So even if you don't understand what a passage means, it helps to simply state, in your own words, what it says. Some versions of the Bible are paraphrased versions and can be helpful in this process.

Step #4 – Pulverize. The secret to good Bible study is a matter of asking appropriate questions of the text. Bombard the text with as many questions as you can think of related to the text. When you pulverize something you break into small chunks. You can do this in Bible study by identifying key words or phrases that need definition. Ask why certain words were chosen by the writer. Ask why some things were not stated in the text. Note words or phrases that are repeated. Use of an analytical concordance can provide definitions for words based on the original language of the text (Greek, Hebrew or Aramaic).

Step #5 – Personalize. Now you are getting closer to understanding what God is saying in the text, and specifically what God is saying *to you.* There may be a command that God wants you to obey, or a promise He wants you to claim, or a peril He wants you to avoid. Is there anything about the truth you have studied that relates directly or indirectly to anything you may be going through at the time? Watch carefully. Sometimes God gives a promise, not for you, but for someone you will encounter that day who needs encouragement or direction.

Step #6 – Praise. Remember, each time you open your Bible you are having an encounter with God. You will discover things about God that are worthy of praise. Take time to praise and thank God for how He has revealed Himself and how He has acted in history and eternity. In several places in the Bible the Lord reveals Himself by different names. Most of us are known by one name, and the purpose of that name is strictly for identification. In biblical times a person's name was more than an identifying tag for them; it was synonymous with their character. So God is revealed by scores of different names in the Bible because no one name can ultimately capture the essence of His character. When you come across these names of God in the Bible, they provide a rich occasion for praise and adoration of the Lord.

Step #7 – Prayer. Our time in the word of God is bracketed by prayer at the beginning and the end. Ask God to cause His word to transform your life. When the Holy Spirit brings conviction of sin through a text of Scripture, stop and confess that sin immediately. Repent and commit to walk away from that path of evil. Claim any appropriate promises that God shows you in your time with Him in His Word. Again, the purpose of Bible reading and study is not just to gain information ... it is to experience transformation. As the Lord reveals His will to you in His Word, express in prayer your desire to obey His will.

Take Away for Today: As you have spent time with God in His Word today, cling to what He has spoken to you. Reflect on it though the day. Share it with others.

PART II ~ DAY 5
MEMORIZING AND MEDITATING ON
GOD'S WORD

Today's Scripture Reading: Psalm 1:1-6

Words have a way of sticking with us through a day, or even longer. Think of the last time someone complimented you on the way you were dressed, or the way you handled an assignment at work. Didn't those words stick with you through the day ... or even longer? Or think also about the last time someone criticized you for something. Those critical words may have lodged so tenaciously in your brain that you couldn't stop thinking about them. You rehearsed those painful words over and over again. Those words, whether positive or negative, affected your mood for the rest of the day.

Envision your mind being dominated each day by biblical thoughts that came to you in your time alone with God in His Word? Envision those thoughts being so strong that they crowd out other less worthy, less wholesome thoughts that usually swirl around in your head.

The Bible instructs us in this way about our thoughts:

"Finally, brothers, whatever is true, whatever is noble, whatever is right, whatever is pure, whatever is lovely, whatever is admirable—if anything is excellent or praiseworthy—think about such things" (Philippians 4:8).

Through the years I have found it extremely helpful to make Scripture memory part of my devotional time. I'll memorize portions of God's Word and use part of my devotional time each day to meditate upon and review the verses I'm memorizing. I particularly like this approach because it trains me to not only hide God's Word in my heart, but also to think deeply about their meaning for my life.

The Psalmist says of the blessed man (and woman): "His delight is in the law of the Lord, and on his law he meditates day and night" (Psalm 1:2). The Psalmist also observes: "How can a young man keep his way pure? By living according to your word. I seek you with all my heart; do not let me stray from your commands. I have hidden your word in my heart that I might not sin against you" (Psalm 119:9-11).

Robert Morgan, in his book *100 Bible Verses (Everyone Should Know by Heart)*, likens memorizing Scripture to "going on a shopping spree for the mind, a chance to collect and store up treasures you'll enjoy for years." [14]

Morgan continues his assessment of the value of Scripture memory: "Though it's as easy as repeating words aloud, it's as powerful as acorns dropping into furrows in the forest. It makes the Bible portable; you can take it with you everywhere without packing it in purse or briefcase. It makes Scripture accessible day and night. It allows God's Word to sink into your brain and permeate your subconscious and even your unconscious thoughts. It gives you a word to say to anyone, in season and out of season. It fills your heart and home with the best thoughts ever recorded. It saturates the personality, satiates the soul, and stockpiles the mind. It changes the atmosphere of every family and alters the weather forecast of every day." [15]

There are numerous benefits to memorizing Scripture. In Psalm 19 David extols the great value of imbedding God's word in our lives:

It gives us victory over sin. In Psalm 119:9 the psalmist asks the question: "How can a young man keep his way pure?" The answer follows: "By living according to (God's) word." In v.11 he goes on to say, "I have hidden your word in my heart that I might not sin against you." Jesus withstood the vicious assaults of Satan in the Wilderness of Temptation by answering each temptation with Scripture which He most assuredly had memorized.

It gives us wisdom. "The statutes of the Lord are trustworthy, making wise the simple" (Psalm 19:7b). Life's way is often treacherous. The wisdom we need to stay on the right path is found in God's Word. Scripture stored in our memory banks provides wisdom for the many decisions we have to make throughout each day. Jesus said, "Everyone who hears these words of mine and puts them into practice is like a wise man..." (Matthew 7:24).

It shapes our thinking around biblical truth. The life God envisions for us is that we might be "conformed to the likeness of his Son" (Romans 8:29). Conforming to the likeness of God's Son starts with the renewing or changing of our mind. "Do not conform any longer to the pattern of this world, but be transformed by the renewing of your mind. Then you will be able to test and approve what God's will is—his good, pleasing and perfect will" (Romans 12:2).

It enhances our ministry to others. "Let the word of Christ dwell in you richly as you teach and admonish one another with all wisdom..." (Colossians 3:16). As God's Word is at home in our lives we are able to minister to others most effectively. Scripture committed to memory can be easily shared with a fellow believer who needs encouragement or with a non-believer who needs a witness about Jesus Christ.

It is a platform for meditation. True Christian meditation is a lost art today. It has been hijacked by other religions or by quasi-spiritual practices. Done properly, however, biblical meditation is an age-old discipline that pays rich spiritual dividends. It was to a busy military leader named Joshua that the Lord gave this counsel: "Do not let this Book of the Law depart from your mouth; meditate on it day and night, so that you may be careful to do everything written in it. Then you will be prosperous and successful" (Joshua 1:8).

Let's drill down a little deeper on the twin disciplines of Scripture memorization and meditation. Moses told Joshua that his success in life was dependent upon his internalization of the Word of God. The Word of God ("this Book of the Law") was not to depart from Joshua's mouth. In other words, it was to be continuously on his lips. That would be the case because he had internalized the Word in his life. He would slow down enough to spend time thinking deeply about the things of God. Memorization allowed Joshua to do this "day and night." As a result Joshua would have the requisite wisdom to carry out his God-given assignment with success.

Psalm 1 speaks of the man of God in this way: "His *delight* is in the law of the Lord, and on his law he meditates day and night (Psalm 1:2, italics mine). A similar expression is found in Psalm 119:97 where the psalmist says, "Oh, how I *love* your law! I meditate on it all day long" (italics mine). From a positive perspective we tend to meditate on and to think deeply about things we love. As I write, our family has just returned from a delightful vacation together in the beauty of Yellowstone National Park. I find myself reliving enjoyable moments with my children and grandchildren in the magnificence of God's great creation. Scriptural meditation is the same. It is an expression of our love for and our delight in the Word of God.

Take Away for Today: Start with a verse with which you may already be familiar. Use the alarm on your phone, or some other trigger, to cause you to stop for a moment, review the verse, and think about how the truth is helping you this day.

Part III
Envision ... Obeying God

ENVISION: You live in such a love relationship with Jesus that you are obedient to Him in all things. Self-denial opens the door to whatever Christ calls upon you to do. You avoid situations in which you might be tempted to think, do or say sinful things. When you realize some part of your life is not square with the commands of the Lord, you immediately move to bring them into line. You lament your sin and readily confess and repent. There is no difference between your public life and your private life. The gap between what you profess and the way you actually live is diminishing. You routinely choose God's way. You regularly employ spiritual disciplines as a means of "training for godliness." Holiness, more than happiness, is becoming the supreme goal of life for you. The indwelling Spirit of God has complete control of your life as you yield to Him moment by moment through each day. You strive to consistently follow the teachings of God's Word and the leading of His Holy Spirit.

SCRIPTURAL FOUNDATION: Luke 9:23-26; John 14:15; 15:10; Romans 12:1-2; I Corinthians 10:13; II Corinthians 7:1; Colossians 3:5-10; I Timothy 4:7-8; Titus 2:12-14; I Peter 2:11

Part III ~ Day 1
Obeying God

Today's Scripture Reading: John 14:15-21

We don't read and study the Bible merely for information. We read and study it for transformation. Ultimately it is intended to affect the way we think and act. It isn't enough for us to read, study, memorize and meditate on God's Word if we do not ultimately do what it says.

The Apostle James gives a vivid image of what obedience looks like: "Do not merely listen to the word, and so deceive yourselves. Do what it says" (James 1:22). James goes on to say that a person who hears the Word of God but doesn't do what it says is like a man who looks at himself in a mirror. Having seen something about himself in the mirror that obviously needs to be corrected, he simply walks away forgetting what he has seen. It would be like you looking in the mirror and seeing a piece of spinach left in your teeth from lunch, but instead of removing it you simply ignore it and go on your way.

God's Word is a mirror that, among other things, detects and reflects any sin in our lives. The right response to that is that we admit it, confess it, repent of it and go a different direction.

So we are alerted to the fact that it is possible for one to "merely listen to the word." This easily happens when we read and study the Bible for information and not transformation. The life God envisions for us is an everyday life fully riveted to the truth of God's Word. This life is what we were created for from the beginning, and it is filled with purpose and power.

Following Jesus requires obedience to Him. Jesus said, "If you hold to my teaching, you are really my disciples. Then you will know the truth, and the truth will set you free" (John 8:31-32). So the key to this glorious life of truth and freedom is entered through obedience ("holding") to the commands of Christ.

Because we, as believers, still struggle with our own sin nature, any call to obey Christ will be difficult for us. Our sin nature rebels against the commands of God. Jesus understood this when He said, "If anyone would come after me, he must deny himself and take up his cross and follow me" (Matthew 16:24). Jesus anticipates that the life to which He calls us is great beyond our wildest dreams, but it will require denying our own agendas and desires.

This matter of obedience to the Father and His Son has been grossly misunderstood. We often think that God has arbitrarily set rules we are to follow, and they have nothing to do with our relationship with Him. We might even go so far as to think that God is playing a cruel cosmic game with us to try to see if He can trick us into messing up. A popular game during my childhood days was a game called "Simon Says." One person was designated as Simon. Simon would call out commands such as "take one step forward," or "raise your right hand." However, the trick was that Simon must first say, "Simon says…" For example if Simon issued a command to raise your right hand and you did so, you would be out because the command was not preceded by "Simon says…" On the other hand if the command was "Simon says raise your right hand" and you obeyed, you stayed in the game for the next round.

Many people have given up on the Christian faith because they see God as a cosmic "Simon" in heaven issuing meaningless commands and hoping to trick us into failure. Nothing could be farther from the truth of authentic Christianity. As a matter of fact Jesus places obedience in the context of a faithful, loving relationship with Himself. Consider the following passages:

"If you love me, you will obey what I command" (John 14:15).

"Whoever has my commands and obeys them, he is the one who loves me. He who loves me will be loved by my Father, and I too will love him and show myself to him" (John 14:21).

"If anyone loves me, he will obey my teaching. My Father will love him, and we will come to him and make our home with him. He who does not love me will not obey my teaching. These words you hear are not my own; they belong to the Father who sent me" (John 14:23-24).

God has created us for Himself and He knows that His will is ultimately what is best for us. So God's call to obedience to His commands is rooted in His loving desire for us to experience His best for our life. To fail to obey His commands places us in great jeopardy. In His great Sermon on the Mount, Jesus encouraged His followers: "Therefore everyone who hears these words of mine and puts them into practice is like a wise man who built his house on the rock. The rain came down, the streams rose, and the winds blew and beat against that house; yet it did not fall, because it had its foundation on the rock" (Matthew 7:24-25).

Not long ago, a friend of mine posted this question on Facebook: "What would happen if we began to obey everything Jesus commanded?" He received many interesting comments in response. One Facebook friend replied, "Are you crazy? Obeying everything Jesus commanded is impossible."

Jesus could not have made it any clearer. In some of His last words to His disciples Jesus clearly spelled out how His work was to be carried on after He ascended back to heaven: "Then Jesus came to them and said, 'All authority in heaven and on earth has been given to me.

Therefore go and make disciples of all nations, baptizing them in the name of the Father and of the Son and of the Holy Spirit, and teaching them to obey everything I have commanded you. And surely I am with you always, to the very end of the age.'" (Matthew 28:18-20).

"Teach them to obey everything I have command-ed..." Does Jesus really mean "everything"? Are we accountable to that degree? Jesus means what He says and says what He means. So if Jesus said to do it, then it must be possible ... in the grace that He gives. Obedience that flows out of sheer human determination brings glory to man. Obedience that is achieved through the strength that God supplies brings glory to Him.

Certainly the demands of discipleship are lofty. And attempted in our own strength obedience to all the commands of Jesus are impossible to achieve. However if we depend upon grace to fully obey the commands of the Lord then with God all things are possible. Bill Hull, in his book *Choose the Life*, observes: "When Jesus said, 'Follow me ... and I will make your fishers of men' (Matt.4:19), James and John dropped their nets and took action. They said yes to his invitation. Faith is real only when there is obedience." [16]

Take Away for Today: Depending on how you categorize them there are hundreds of commands of Jesus in the four gospels and in the Book of Acts. That may seem a bit overwhelming to us. If so, let's start with just three of the towering commands of Jesus: The Great Commandment – love God with all your heart, soul, mind and strength (Matthew 22:37-40); The New Commandment – love one another as Jesus loved us (John 13:34-35), and The Great Commission – go and make disciples of all nations. Work on these and you'll be well on your way to a life of obeying God and denying self.

PART III ~ DAY 2
SELF-DENIAL

Today's Scripture Reading: John 12:23-33

In our quest to obey everything Christ commands we are immediately met with resistance ... and that resistance rises up from within us. Certainly Jesus knows that something in our sinful selves will always resist going His way. He knows that when we determine we will follow Him it will require denying ourselves. This is clear from the manner in which Jesus calls us to follow Him: "Then Jesus said to his disciples, 'If anyone would come after me, he must deny himself and take up his cross and follow me'" (Matthew 16:24).

Something in our sin nature rebels against the Law of God and the demands of Jesus. Though over time some of the battles with self-denial will grow easier, other desires may doggedly hold on. So inevitably the commands of Jesus will run headlong into our sinful desires. Obeying God will always require some measure of denying self.

Contrary to our wishes, there never is a time when God stops confronting our sinful self with His righteous commands. We may reach a level of maturity where some commands of Jesus no longer require a great battle. For instance, early in your Christian life you may have struggled with profanity. Over time, however, you found it no burden at all to obey Jesus and simply let your "yes" be "yes" and your "no" be "no" (see Matthew 5:37).

Having overcome that habit the Holy Spirit may begin to put His finger on another area of disobedience you had never discovered. It may relate to anger (Matthew 5:21-26) or lust (Matthew 5:27-30) or doing good things to be seen by others (Matthew 6:1). Rest assured that God will be about this pruning work in our lives until the day we die.

This self-denial is at the very heart of the life Jesus envisions for us. It is at this heart of *His* very life. It is likened to dying to one's self. Jesus said, "I tell you the truth, unless a kernel of wheat falls to the ground and dies, it remains only a single seed. But if it dies, it produces many seeds" (John 12:24).

As Jesus marched courageously toward His crucifixion He knew exactly what the Father had in mind. A powerful force was about to be unleashed upon the world that would eventually sweep untold millions into the Kingdom of God. Later in John 12 Jesus said, "I, when I have been lifted up from the earth, will draw all men to myself" (v.32). He was actually speaking about the death He would endure when His body was lifted up on the cross to die one of the cruelest deaths imaginable – death by crucifixion.

This is an important principle in the Christ-life. The gateway to the abundant blessing of God is always through death – not necessarily physical death, but a dying to self and to the world that then paves the way for the awesome activity of God.

Jesus saw Himself as a seed or kernel of wheat that had to fall into the ground and die in order to produce a harvest. Jesus was speaking of the agricultural process where the seed that is sown into the blackness of the earth results in the miraculous process of germination. Soon a little plant sprouts and before long a stalk of grain pushes upward and is crowned with a head filled with countless new seeds – the promise of a multiplied harvest.

Jesus had in mind the great harvest of souls that would come to new life through His self-denying, self-sacrificing action upon the cross. Jesus was, however, not just describing His solitary determination; He was calling His disciples to follow His example in dying to self. Then a great harvest of souls is possible because Christ-followers radically obey Jesus when He commanded, "If anyone would come after me, he must deny himself and take up his cross daily and follow me" (Luke 9:23). Jesus died to His own wishes and submitted to the will of His Father. So we are called to do the same. "He himself bore our sins in his body on the tree, so that we might die to sins and live for righteousness" (1 Peter 2:24).

One facet of self-denial is repentance. When we talk about repentance we typically have in mind the repenting that has to be done before a person is saved. "Repent, then, and turn to God, so that your sins may be wiped out, that times of refreshing may come from the Lord" (Acts 3:19). There are, however, also plenty of instances where believers are called to repent. I think of the words of Jesus to wayward believers: "Those whom I love I rebuke and discipline. So be earnest, and repent" (Revelation 3:19). Biblical repentance is not just feeling bad about sins we have committed and vowing to never do it again. True, biblical repentance is the holy disgust of our sin that leads us to depend on God to forgive and change us. This is at the root of self-denial.

I discovered long ago that this call to obey God and deny self is not burdensome. In fact Jesus calls us away from such a life. He said, "Come to me, all you who are weary and burdened, and I will give you rest" (Matthew 11:28). He was reaching out to people who were tired from the hard toil of and being loaded down with heavy demands of religion. Instead they should come and yoke themselves to Jesus and learn from Him (in short, become a disciple). By doing this they find rest for their souls from the burden of sin. So Jesus calls people to trade their heavy, tiring burdens for His yoke and burden, which in comparison are easy and light (Matthew 11:29-30).

Daily we are faced with the challenge of dying to our own ambitions, amusements and agendas in order to live for righteousness. Unless the kernel of wheat falls into the ground and dies it remains only a single seed. If there is to be any widespread revival that results in great numbers of people coming into the Kingdom of God, it will be as believers take up the "exchanged life" described by the Apostle Paul: "I have been crucified with Christ and I no longer live, but Christ lives in me. The life I live in the body, I live by faith in the Son of God, who loved me and gave himself for me" (Galatians 2:20).

The battle that rages in each of our souls looks like this:

"I'm just too busy to set aside the time to draw near to God in prayer." *Unless a kernel of wheat falls into the ground and dies...*

"My time is precious to me. I will not give up any of it to seriously seek God in His Word." *Unless a kernel of wheat falls into the ground and dies...*

"This secret sin is just too hard to shake; it's just the way I am." *Unless a kernel of wheat falls into the ground and dies...*

"Witnessing? Forget it. I will not risk humiliation over Jesus." *Unless a kernel of wheat falls into the ground and dies...*

"Tithing? That's impossible. I need every cent for my needs and wants." *Unless a kernel of wheat falls into the ground and dies…*

"Fasting? You've got to be kidding! I can't miss a meal." *Unless a kernel of wheat falls into the ground and dies…*

"Sorry, I can't take on that new ministry. I need more time for myself and my family." *Unless a kernel of wheat falls into the ground and dies…*

"I'm afraid if I really get serious about Jesus I won't be accepted by my friends." *Unless a kernel of wheat falls into the ground and dies…*

In 1956 Jim Elliot and four other courageous souls heard the call of God to take the gospel into a dangerous region of Ecuador. Just two days after arriving all five men were dead, having been savagely killed by the Ecuadorian Indians they had gone to reach for Christ. Elliot and his colleagues left behind five young widows and nine fatherless children. The blood of these five martyrs became the fuel for the fires of spiritual awakening that broke out in the region. God used their witness, and the witness of their wives who remained in Ecuador to reach the people who had murdered their husbands.

Some would say it was a waste. Jim Elliott would disagree. In a journal entry six years before his death Jim Elliot wrote: "He is no fool who gives what he cannot keep to gain that which he cannot lose." [17]

Jesus always speaks truth. "Unless a kernel of wheat falls into the ground and dies, it remains only a single seed. But if it dies, it produces many seeds."

Take Away for Today: Rejoice when the demands of Jesus call you to deny yourself in a certain area. Know that in that event Christ is pulling you more tightly into His orbit to where everything in your life revolves around Him.

Part III ~ Day 3
Loving God vs. Loving the World

Today's Scripture Reading: I John 2:15-17

As we strive toward the life God envisions for us there is this inner struggle with sin and self that rages in every soul. Allow me to approach the issue from a slightly different angle. The Apostle John admonished his early readers in this way: *"Do not love the world or anything in the world. If anyone loves the world, the love of the Father is not in him"* (I John 2:15).

So, again, a continuous battle rages *in* the heart of every believer … and *for* the heart of every believer. The battle is over which love reigns supreme in the believer's heart. Is it the love of the world or the love of the Father?

This boils down to how we are inwardly sustained in our everyday lives. As we go through the day are we sustained by clinging to and cherishing the "world," or are we sustained by clinging to and cherishing the Father? The two loves cannot exist alongside each other. At any given moment we are either finding life in the world or we are finding it in the Father. If we strive to fill our thirsty souls through the love of the world, the love of the Father is not filling us.

So what exactly does it mean to "love the world"? Don't misunderstand this to say that we are not to love the *people* of the world. God loves the people of the world (John 3:16), and so should we. What John is describing here is loving the *ways* of the world. The world, then, is the system of values and goals which excludes God and appeals to the sinful nature.

John goes on to explain: "For everything in the world—the cravings of sinful man, the lust of his eyes and the boasting of what he has and does—comes not from the Father but from the world" (1 John 2:16).

The "cravings of sinful man" are the sinful desires that seethe within our sin nature. The "lust of the eyes" describes our covetous tendency to acquire more and more. The "boasting of what he has and does" points to pridefully seeking the notice of others for what we have accumulated and accomplished.

These three manifestations of the love of the world are very powerful in the human soul. They are deceiving in that they entice us to find our sense of inner well-being from these worldly passions and desires. And at least for a season, these passions and desires make us *think* we are happy; but it doesn't last long. Our hearts are restless and will never be satisfied by the things of the world.

The opposite of this is being sustained and finding

our inner sense of well-being from the "love of the Father." Our heavenly Father's love is the only thing that will quench the thirsting of our souls. The Father's love is unconditional, all-encompassing and altogether satisfying. His love is steadfast and never ceasing. Like the rays from the sun, God's love is always coming at us.

The love of the Father is very real and experiential. We feel it. We are strengthened by it. It fills our innermost beings with eternal delight. The Psalmist describes it this way: "Because your love is better than life, my lips will glorify you" (Psalm 63:3). Imagine being able to say to God, "Your love is better than life to me."

Our love for God flows from obedience to the will of the Father. As we live each day committed to following His commands we are acknowledging that it is His love, not the things of the world that ultimately sustains us.

The love of the world will never satisfy us because it is transitory. John says, "The world and its desires pass away..." (I John 2:17). We know this instinctively when we sense the shallow, fleeting nature of the pleasures of the world ... how they don't really satisfy deeply or in a lasting way.

However, "the man who does the will of God lives forever" (v.17). In faithfully obeying the will of God we are expressing our complete dependence upon the Lord. Doing his will means we value His pleasure more than we value the pleasures of this world. As we obey there is something eternal about the joy it brings. "Living forever" means *really* living.

The "love of the world" may provide momentary pleasure but it always runs down and leaves with only a cheap, hollow thrill. The "love of the Father" is never-ending and intensifies right up to the time when we are ushered into the presence of unimaginable joy in the presence of God for eternity.

The gospels record for us how Jesus faced an onslaught of temptation from Satan (see Matthew 4:1-11). Having spent forty days alone fasting in the wilderness Satan approached Jesus with at least three alluring temptations, each similar to the "love of the world" described by John. Of course, our Lord did not possess a sin nature as we do, but the temptations were just as real and powerful due to the hideous designs of Satan. Jesus resisted each temptation by recalling Scriptural truth. The "love of the Father" sustained Jesus through the ordeal of temptation.

Sin and Satan vie for control of our lives. We are assaulted with every imaginable lie intended to wrest control of our lives from God. Truly the most common way temptation enters our lives is through thoughts in our minds. If Satan can get us to believe and dwell on lies, he has pushed our lives into a deadly dive toward destruction.

Just think about how real this is:

- We falsely believe that someone is out to hurt us; we begin to plot how we can hurt them first.
- An attractive person, not our mate, comes into our field of vision and we begin to imagine sexual intimacy with them. Lust is conceived that easily gives birth to sin.
- A godless, materialistic worldview begins to capture our thinking. We soon begin to doubt the love of God and the life to which He has called us. Our mind becomes a dark cellar where sin thrives.

Read how the Apostle Paul describes the battle: "For the weapons of our warfare are not of the flesh but have divine power to destroy strongholds. We destroy arguments and every lofty opinion raised against the knowledge of God, and take every thought captive to obey Christ" (2 Corinthians 10:4-5 ESV).

So make sure you have control of the cockpit of your life … the mind. Realize you are in a battle not against visible forces, but against invisible evil forces. Satan and his demons are hard at work to supplant the truth of God with the lies of evil. Take every thought captive to the obedience of Christ. Fill your mind with the truth and wisdom of God's Word. Dwell on it throughout each day. The battle is won one thought at a time.

Ultimately we must remember that as we seek to obey God and deny self we are not powerless in the face of temptation. "No temptation has seized you except what is common to man. And God is faithful; he will not let you be tempted beyond what you can bear. But when you are tempted, he will also provide a way out so that you can stand up under it" (1 Corinthians 10:13).

This single verse has provided believers with spiritual wisdom and encouragement in the face of vicious temptations. Notice that temptation alone is not sin. Though Jesus was sinless He was, nonetheless, tempted in every way we are. We are not alone in the battle. Temptations are "common to man." Satan does not have complete sovereignty in the experience of temptation. God will not allow the evil one to tempt you beyond what you are able to withstand through the power of God. There will always be a way of escape. The big question is this: "Are you willing to take the way of escape provided by God?"

Take Away for Today: Make a conscience effort throughout this day to focus on the love of God. Allow that love to sustain you in the face of the fierce temptations to cave in to the temptations of Satan and the love of the world.

PART III ~ DAY 4
TRAINING FOR GODLINESS

Today's Scripture Reading: I Timothy 4:6-8

A powerful image used repeatedly by New Testament writers has to do with the world of athletics, popular in the ancient world. For example the Apostle Paul wrote to his young preacher friend Timothy: "Train yourself to be godly. For physical training is of some value, but godliness has value for all things, holding promise for both the present life and the life to come" (I Timothy 4:7-8). The athlete must exercise discipline in his training in order to compete successfully in the games. He does not simply *try* to win; he *trains* to win.

Several years ago I decided that I needed to find a consistent way to stay physically fit. I'm not sure what possessed me to do it, but I determined that running would be a good way to accomplish that goal. I was on the track team in high school, but I hated the long distance races. To my surprise I found running a few miles was not as bad as I remembered it. Now, several half-marathon and marathon races later, I've actually come to love it. (I know that sounds sick, but it's true!)

In the course of training for and running long-distances I've learned that a runner doesn't just simply go out one day and *try* to run 13.1 or 26.2 miles. Failure is certain, at least for most mortals. If a person seriously wants to run a half or full marathon they must train to do so. That means they start running short distances at a very slow pace. Gradually over time they add distance and intensity to their runs. It's amazing how the human body, otherwise healthy, adapts to the increased demands of conditioning. So when race day comes the runner is able go out and successfully run the long-distance, not just because they *tried* to do but because they *trained* to do it.

The Bible says that spiritual training ... training for godliness ... operates the same way. The word "godliness" means serious piety toward God. Titus 2:12 says that God's grace "teaches us to say 'No' to ungodliness and worldly passions, and to live self-controlled, upright and godly lives in this present age."

That kind of life – to live self-controlled, upright and godly lives in this present age – requires discipline. The Greek word translated "train" in I Timothy 4:7 is the word from which we get our "gymnasium." What went on in the Roman gymnasium was disciplined training for athletic competition. The point Paul is making is that entering into the life of godliness requires spiritual workouts. Like running a race, we don't *try* to be godly; we *train* to be godly.

The church in Corinth was located near the site of the

famous Isthmian Games (a forerunner of modern Olympic Games). To them Paul wrote: "Everyone who competes in the games goes into strict training. They do it to get a crown that will not last; but we do it to get a crown that will last forever. Therefore I do not run like a man running aimlessly; I do not fight like a man beating the air. No, I beat my body and make it my slave so that after I have preached to others, I myself will not be disqualified for the prize" (1 Corinthians 9:25-27).

The writer of Hebrews picks up on the same theme: "Therefore, since we are surrounded by such a great cloud of witnesses, let us throw off everything that hinders and the sin that so easily entangles, and let us run with perseverance the race marked out for us" (Hebrews 12:1).

We are to run "the race." What an interesting way to describe the life God envisions for us in Christ. In the original language, the word for "race" is the word from which we get our word "agony." Certainly the life to which God has called us is filled with untold blessings, but it is still a contest and a struggle. It is not that we are competing against others; it is that we are striving to bring all of our being under the Lordship of Jesus Christ. That, as we all know, is a continuous struggle.

We are to run the race with perseverance ... with patient endurance. We keep running, even when everything inside us says, "Quit!" As a runner some days it's a challenge to keep going; other days it's a challenge just to get started. I often run with a group of runners on Saturday mornings, and typically I have to be out the door by about 6:00am. Many mornings when the alarm goes off, I have this conversation with myself: "Maybe I can just sleep in today. I'll get my run in later in the day (fat chance!). I haven't missed a run in weeks; I deserve a break." Then I think: "If I bail out today, it will be much easier to bail out next week. That's the way bad habits get started." Somehow I manage to drag my lazy bones out of the bed, climb into my running shoes and hit the road.

Again, we don't *try* to be godly; we *train* to be godly.

For many years I learned that my devotional life should consist of reading God's Word and praying. And this is certainly true. Reading and studying God's Word is the primary way God speaks to us. Praying is the primary way we speak to God (though He also speaks to us in prayer). Years ago, however, I came to understand that there are other ways to experience the life of Christ that help me to grow spiritually. These are commonly called "spiritual disciplines." Think of them as holy habits that position us to experience the transformation God envisions for our lives. Or, they are the spiritual workouts by which we regularly exercise in order to train for godliness.

Now you may think, "Oh no, another discipline for me to keep up with. I'm already so undisciplined in my life. One more discipline to add to my list is going to push me over the edge to more guilt and frustration." I couldn't agree more, if we're thinking of disciplines as another rule to add to the list of things I have to do (or not do).

Still others look at spiritual disciplines, or at least a faulty understanding of the disciplines, and object that they are simply ways to try to please God. The more disciplined we are in various ways, the more pleasing we are to God. That's not the proper motivation for the disciplines.

Certainly God is opposed to *earning* His pleasure in our salvation. God is not, however, opposed to *effort* in our growth in Christ, as long as those efforts flow out of our experience of the grace of God at work in our lives. Remember, Titus 2:12 says that God's grace "teaches us to say 'No' to ungodliness and worldly passions, and to live self-controlled, upright and godly lives in this present age." So grace-fueled effort is involved in living out the Christ-life.

However, what if we were to understand spiritual disciplines as habits that will strengthen our walk with Christ? I like Jim Wilson's definition of spiritual disciplines. They are, "small things Christians intentionally do to open themselves to God's work of conforming them to the image of Christ." [18] Wilson links spiritual disciplines to the process of spiritual formation, which he defines as "God's work of changing a believer into the likeness of Jesus by creating a new identity in Christ and by empowering a lifelong relationship of love, trust and obedience to glorify God." [19]

Or to put it in the words of Richard Foster, "The classical Disciplines of the spiritual life call us to move beyond surface living into the depths." [20] The disciplines allow us to place ourselves before God in such a way that He can transform us. They are a means of opening ourselves to God's grace which alone can bring about that transformation from the inside out.

An important biblical principle for the Christian life is this: "The one who sows to please his sinful nature, from that nature will reap destruction; the one who sows to please the Spirit, from the Spirit will reap eternal life" (Galatians 6:8). Richard Foster explains how this fits into the discussion of spiritual disciplines: "A farmer is helpless to grow grain; all he can do is to provide the right conditions for the growing of grain. He puts the seed in the ground where the natural forces take over and up comes the grain. That is the way with the Spiritual Disciplines – they are a way of sowing to the Sprit. The disciplines are God's way of getting us into the ground; they put us where He can work within us and transform us. By themselves the Spiritual Disciplines can do nothing; they can only get us to the place where something can be done." [21]

While many writers have attempted to list the various spiritual disciplines that have been practiced by believers through the ages, a few of the more commonly utilized disciplines are:

- Study
- Solitude

- Fasting
- Prayer
- Service
- Worship
- Simplicity

The spiritual disciplines are real ways in which we utilize our body in obeying God and denying self. They result in glory to God and good for us. Godliness, Paul tells us, "has value for all things, holding promise for both the present life and the life to come" (1 Timothy 4:8).

Take Away for Today: Whether it's meeting God for your devotional time, or attending church, or showing up for a prayer group, or for a ministry responsibility, the battle with self rages every day. Will you bail out today, or will you discipline yourself to keep running with perseverance. When everything inside you says "Quit!" the indwelling Spirit of Jesus and the great cloud of faithful witnesses shout to you, "Go!"

PART III ~ DAY 5
THE ROLE OF THE HOLY SPIRIT

Today's Scripture Reading: John 16:5-15

I cannot leave this section without affirming the role of the Holy Spirit in this matter of living the life God envisions for us. All we are called to be and do in Christ is accomplished through His indwelling Spirit. God doesn't just dream of this kind of life happening in those whom He has created. He is active in the process through our eternal redemption and through the gift of the Holy Spirit. When I encourage us to "envision the life" I am in no way implying that simply by envisioning it we can make it happen. It is, after all, the very life of Christ in us made real and experiential through the ministry of His Holy Spirit.

So let's think about what the Bible says about our relationship to the Holy Spirit and His part in making the life of Christ real in us. The deep change that God intends for those whom He redeems happens through the instrumentality of the Word of God and the Spirit of God.

The walls of the mountain home where I am writing today are laced with yards and yards of electrical wiring.

Pulsating through those wires is electrical power sufficient to do amazing things. However I have the option of sitting in a dark room with no light turned on. I have the option of sitting at a powerless computer which I have not plugged into the power outlet in the wall. I have the option of eating raw food because I have not turned on the power to the microwave. You get the point. There is power pulsating all around me, but I have no connection, no relationship with that power until I access it. I must flip a switch or plug a plug into an electrical outlet. Then all the power of electricity is at my disposal. I can do things through that power than I cannot do in my own strength.

The same thing is true with the power of the Holy Spirit. The power of the Holy Spirit is the energy on which the Christ-life runs. Apart from that energy this life simply doesn't happen. Remember Jesus' promise to His followers upon His ascension to the right hand of the Father in heaven: "But you will receive power when the Holy Spirit comes on you; and you will be my witnesses in Jerusalem, and in all Judea and Samaria, and to the ends of the earth" (Acts 1:8).

Let me walk you through the basics of our relationship with the Holy Spirit by which we access this energy for the life God envisions for us. The Spirit reveals Christ and His teachings (John 14:26; 16:8-11). He is the agent of regeneration in believers (Titus 3:5-6). The Holy Spirit indwells all believers (I Corinthians 6:19) and immerses believers in the life of Christ (Matthew 3:11). The indwelling Spirit is God's seal of ownership on us (II Corinthians 1:22). He is the instrument by which the process of sanctification takes place in us (II Thessalonians 2:13). The love of God becomes real in our experience through the ministry of the Holy Spirit. "God has poured out his love into our hearts by the Holy Spirit, whom he has given us" (Romans 5:5). Ultimately the Spirit will be the catalyst for our bodily resurrection at the second coming of Christ (see Romans 8:11).

As it is with the Father and with the Son, we may have a relationship with the Holy Spirit. The Bible spells out how we maintain that relationship with the Spirit:

Be consciously filled with the Spirit. "Be filled with the Spirit" (Ephesians 5:18b). This is a command to be continuously surrendered to the control and influence of the Holy Spirit.

Be led by the Spirit. "Those who are led by the Spirit of God are sons of God" (Romans 8:14). The word "led" means to be taken or carried along by the Spirit.

Let your mind be controlled by the Spirit. "Those who live in accordance with the Spirit have their minds set on what the Spirit desires" (Romans 8:5b). The guidance of the Holy Spirit is to dominate our thinking throughout the day.

Pray guided by the Spirit. "Pray in the Holy Spirit" (Jude 20b). I take this to mean that we pray with the pervasive assistance of the Holy Spirit.

Live by the Spirit. "Live by the Spirit, and you will not gratify the desires of the sinful nature" (Galatians 5:16). When we live by the Spirit we will display the fruit of the Spirit (Galatians 5:22-23), which is the opposite of the desires of the sinful nature.

Don't grieve the Spirit. "Do not grieve the Holy Spirit of God, with whom you were sealed for the day of redemption" (Ephesians 4:30). Amazingly the Spirit of God feels sorrow when relationships among believers are marked by unwholesome talk, bitterness and hatred. (See Ephesians 4:29-32).

Don't quench the Spirit. "Do not put out the Spirit's fire" (1 Thessalonians 5:19). The Spirit's fire blazes when spiritual gifts like prophecy are fully functioning in the church.

Walk in step with the Spirit. "Since we live by the Spirit, let us keep in step with the Spirit" (Galatians 5:25). The picture here is of soldiers walking in a line in step with one another. The Holy Spirit sounds our cadence for us.

The life of a follower of Christ is very much a daily walk with Him. The great challenge of the Christian life is to maintain that consistent walk with the Lord. The goal is to live every waking moment in step with His Spirit dwelling within us.

I realize that this is such an elusive concept for us that it is hard to know exactly how this looks or feels. How do I know when I am walking in step with the Spirit? It is very much a matter of spiritual concentration and focus. And it can and should be maintained as we are going about the daily tasks of life at home, at work, at school, and everywhere our daily traffic pattern takes us.

John Wesley was instrumental in the great revival that swept through the British Isles in the middle part of the 18th century. Fortunately John Wesley kept a daily journal that chronicles, in brief descriptions, the intensity of his daily walk with God. His journals have been a great source of inspiration for serious followers of Christ for over 300 years. On one occasion I had the privilege of visiting John Wesley's Chapel in Bristol, England. On display there were pages from his journal. Two journal entries from December, 1740 caught my attention:

"Sun.23 – While I was reading prayers at Snow-fields, I found such light and strength as I never remember to have had before. I saw every thought, as well as action or word, just as it was rising in my heart; and whether it was right with God, or tainted with pride or selfishness. I never knew before (I mean not as at this time) what it was 'to be still before God.'

"Mon.24 – I walked by the Grace of God, in the same spirit; and about eight (o'clock), being with two or three that believed in Jesus, I felt such an awe and tender sense of the presence of God as greatly confirmed me therein: So that God was before me all day long. I sought and found him in every place; and could truly say, when I lay down at night, 'Now I have <u>lived</u> a day.'"

Wesley describes for us what it means to live each waking moment in unbroken communion with God. Again, I notice the concentration and focus that enabled him, throughout a busy schedule, to live in the light of God's tender presence. He monitors every thought, action and word in light of will of the Lord. This must have been what David had in mind when he said, "I have set the Lord always before me; because he is at my right hand, I shall not be shaken" (Psalm 16:8 ESV).

This is very much an active thing. Wesley *found* the Lord in every place because He *sought* the Lord in every place. Consequently when that day was over and he rested his head on his pillow he was able to say with deep joy, "Now I have lived a day."

When you are interrupted by someone does the very real presence of the Lord, by His Spirit, govern your response? When you are faced with a temptation does the very real presence of the Lord, by His Spirit, strengthen your will? When you are changing a dirty diaper does the very real presence of the Lord, by His Spirit, give meaning to that moment? When you are presented with the opportunity to minister or witness to another does the very real presence of the Lord, by His Spirit, propel you forward on mission for Him? When you sit down to a delicious meal does the very real presence of God, by His Spirit, cause you to instantly pause to thank Him? Imagine the abiding joy of coming to the end of the day, resting your head on your pillow and thinking, "Now I have *lived* a day!"

Take Away for the Day: Allow me to place this vision before you – that you could begin to measure the success of any given day in terms of how well you stayed focused on the presence of the Lord, by His Spirit, that day.

PART IV
ENVISION ... SERVING GOD AND OTHERS

ENVISION: Your life is humbly aligned with the will of God. Daily you respond to God's call to be His holy servant on mission with Him. You understand your unique spiritual giftedness and have identified the grace gifts that have been deposited by the Holy Spirit in your life. You are utilizing those gifts for building up the Body of Christ and demonstrating God's love to all people. You are energized and empowered by the Holy Spirit to serve God in the strength that He supplies. You are involved in at least one meaningful responsibility of service in the church as well as beyond the church in the community. Everything you have has been fully and joyfully surrendered to God. You generously contribute to the financial needs of your local church and the worldwide Kingdom of God.

SCRIPTURAL FOUNDATION: Matthew 25:14-29; Mark 10:43-45; John 13:34-35; I Corinthians 12:4-11; Galatians 5:13-14; Philippians 2:3-8; I John 3:16

PART IV ~ DAY 1
OUR EXAMPLE IN SERVICE

Today's Scripture Reading: Mark 10:32-45

The life God envisions for us is altogether joyous and blessed, not because God is obligated to make us happy, but because in this life we discover the tremendous joy of serving God and others. What inspires this kind of self-lessness in service?

Worshippers at our church have the opportunity each Sunday to share prayer requests and praise reports with us. The requests are prayed over by our staff each week. One of those prayer slips, submitted by a child, caught my attention. The little girl wrote: *Praise: My dad ... ministered to a hitchhiker on the way back from the bank, took him to breakfast, watched him eat while drinking a cup of coffee, gave him $10 and dropped him off at a homeless shelter.*

I pondered this hand-written note. I imagined the daughter sitting in the backseat silently watching as her dad pulled over to the side of the road and picked up the hitchhiker. No detail escaped her impressionable mind. Her eyes were fixed on her dad who compassionately sat in a restaurant with a hungry stranger while he enjoyed a free breakfast. She keenly observed as Dad slipped the man $10 as he dropped him off at a shelter where he would have a warm bed for the night.

The little girl understood something powerful was going on with her father and the stranger. Dad "ministered" to the man, she surmised. She caught the important detail that her dad was doing all this, not just as a good deed, but as a ministry in the name of his Lord.

This precious child learned something more powerful than any sermon I will ever preach. She benefitted from the awesome power of the positive example of a godly parent. The image of her father's service to the hitchhiker will likely stay branded in her soul for many years to come. It will come to her mind when a stranger crosses her path in the years to come. She will know exactly what to do!

As inspiring as that example may be, as Christ-followers our service is inspired by a far greater example … the example of our glorious Lord Jesus Christ. He said, "For even the Son of Man did not come to be served, but to serve, and to give his life as a ransom for many" (Mark 10:45).

Jesus came to this earth to serve, and He demonstrated that in numerous ways. Every touch of Jesus was a serving touch that healed and helped. Every word of Jesus was a serving word that taught, encouraged and enlightened.

On the day before He was crucified Jesus invited His followers to share in the Passover meal with Him. Can you imagine the shock when they walked into the house and found Jesus dressed as a slave prepared to wash the dirty feet of the disciples? This common, menial task was usually reserved for the lowliest slave, but then the Son of Almighty God knelt before each of them, took their filthy feet in His hands and tenderly washed them. Jesus then used this occasion to coach His followers about the importance of serving others: "Now that I, your Lord and Teacher, have washed your feet, you also should wash one another's feet. I have set you an example that you should do as I have done for you. I tell you the truth, no servant is greater than his master, nor is a messenger greater than the one who sent him" (John 13:14-16).

Ironically, Luke in his gospel account recorded that immediately after this Jesus overheard His disciples fussing with one another about which of them was the greatest. How could the disciples, having witnessed such selfless service from their Master, talk about wanting to be the "greatest"? With the embarrassed disciples before Him Jesus redefined greatness in this way: "The greatest among you should be like the youngest, and the one who rules like the one who serves. For who is greater, the one who is at the table or the one who serves? Is it not the one who is at the table? But I am among you as one who serves" (Luke 22:26-27).

It is in the cross of Jesus Christ that we see the supreme example of selfless service to God and to others.

Of course, the crucifixion of Jesus was more than just a good example of self-sacrifice. Indeed it was that, but the greatest accomplishment was His atoning sacrifice for the sins of humanity. That is what achieved our redemption. But in that great work Jesus' mindset then became our pattern for a life of service. "Your attitude should be the same as that of Christ Jesus: Who, being in very nature God, did not consider equality with God something to be grasped, but made himself nothing, taking the very nature of a servant, being made in human likeness. And being found in appearance as a man, he humbled himself and became obedient to death— even death on a cross!" (Philippians 2:5-8).

The service of Christ's death secured redemption for mankind through repentance and faith. And when we follow Jesus into a life of service it is a grand advertise-ment for His love-motivated passion. Jesus anticipated this when He said, "A new command I give you: Love one another. As I have loved you, so you must love one anoth-er. *By this all men will know that you are my disciples,* if you love one another" (John 13:34-35, italics mine).

When we follow our Lord into a life of sacrificial ser-vice others are attracted to our Savior. When they see us giving our lives away for His sake others are challenged to think about what kind of Person would inspire such sacrifice. When they watch us seek first the Kingdom of God and His righteousness, trusting He will supply our every need, others will be challenged to ponder this invisible Kingdom that inspires such hope. Perhaps they will ask "you to give the reason for the hope that you have" (I Peter 3:15).

John Piper observes: "There is no doubt that if we lived more like this, the world would be more likely to consider whether Jesus is an all-satisfying Treasure ... Why don't people ask us about our hope? The answer is probably that we look as if we hope in the same things they do. Our lives don't look like they are on the Calvary road, stripped down for sacrificial love, serving others with the sweet assurance that we don't need to be rewarded in this life. Our reward is great in heaven (Matthew 5:12)!" [22]

In challenging the church at Corinth to serve God and others through their sacrificial giving, the Apostle Paul reminded them: "For you know the grace of our Lord Jesus Christ, that though he was rich, yet for your sakes he became poor, so that you through his poverty might become rich" (II Corinthians 8:9).

Living lives of service to God and others, properly motivated, reflects the glorious gospel of Jesus Christ. As we give of ourselves we are pointing to the One who gave of Himself that we might be saved. He did not come to be served, but to serve and to give His life a ransom for many.

Take Away for Today: As a Christ-follower Jesus lives in you. The One who came to serve, not be served, wants to live His life through you today. Consider every encounter you have with others an opportunity to let Jesus serve them through you.

Part IV ~ Day 2
Grace for Service

Today's Scripture Reading: Ephesians 2:8-10

John MacArthur, in his book *Our Sufficiency in Christ*, tells a story from the life of Charles Haddon Spurgeon. The great preacher was riding home one evening after a heavy day's work, feeling weary and depressed, when the verse came to mind, "My grace is sufficient for you" (II Corinthians 12:9). In his mind he immediately compared himself to a little fish in the Thames River, apprehensive lest drinking so many pints of water in the river each day he might drink the Thames dry. Then Father Thames said to the creature, "Drink away, little fish. My stream is sufficient for you." Next he thought of a little mouse in the granaries of Egypt, afraid lest its daily nibbles exhaust the supplies and cause it to starve to death. Then Joseph came along and said, "Cheer up, little mouse. My granaries are sufficient for you." Then he thought of a man climbing some high mountain to reach its lofty summit and dreading lest his breathing there might exhaust all the oxygen in the atmosphere. The Creator boomed His voice out of heaven, saying, "Breathe away, oh man, and fill your lungs. My atmosphere is sufficient for you!" [23]

Grace is simply the powerful, undeserved, unlimited activity of God in our lives. The life of a Christ-follower runs on grace, like a car runs on gasoline. Everything God calls upon us to be and do is the product of God's grace at work in our lives. Thus as we live each day we ought to consume grace. In a conference I once heard Dallas Willard say, "The saints burn grace like a 747 burns fuel on takeoff, because everything we do is a manifestation of grace."

This only works when we set aside our own sufficiency and dependence on our own strength. The Lord said to Paul in II Corinthians 12:9, "My power is made perfect in weakness." So long as we are full of our confidence and resources there is no room for the grace of God. When we empty ourselves of that self-confidence we leave room for the powerful grace of God to take over.

This is true of our *salvation*. Ephesians 2:8 says, "It is by grace you have been saved, through faith—and this not from yourselves, it is the gift of God…" Salvation isn't accomplished by our good works, but by the powerful, undeserved activity of God in our lives. We appropriate this grace by believing.

This is also true of our *service*. When our lives are sustained by the grace of God what flows from our lives is effective service for God and to others. The Apostle Paul saw his life and ministry in this light: "By the grace of God

I am what I am, and his grace to me was not without effect. No, I worked harder than all of them—yet not I, but the grace of God that was with me" (1 Corinthians 15:10). So grace works. God's grace produces a life of service in the recipients of that grace.

Grace doesn't mean that I just sit back and do nothing. It means that I allow grace to produce in me all that God intends for it to produce. Even my work of service to God and others becomes the product of the grace of God at work.

Hudson Taylor, founder of the China Inland Mission, is one of my spiritual heroes. Feeling the call of God as a teenager to go to China, Taylor obeyed. After having been on the field for about fifteen years, Hudson Taylor felt the weight of the enormous responsibility of leading this missionary enterprise, making him aware that he needed God to do a deeper work in his life. He described his spiritual condition in a letter to his mother:

"My own position becomes continually more and more responsible, and my need greater of special grace to fill it, but I have continually to mourn that I follow at such a distance and learn so slowly to imitate my precious Master. I cannot tell you how I am buffeted sometimes by temptation. I never knew how bad a heart I had. Yet I do know that I love God and love His work, and desire to serve Him only in all things. And I value above all things that precious Savior in Whom alone I can be accepted. Often I am tempted to think that one so full of sin cannot be a child of God at all; but I try to throw it back, and rejoice all the more in the preciousness of Jesus, and in the riches of that grace that has made us 'accepted in the Beloved.' Beloved He is of God; beloved He ought to be of us. But oh, how short I fall here again! May God help me to love Him more and serve Him better. Do pray for me. Pray that the Lord will keep me from sin, will sanctify me wholly, will use me more largely in His service." [24]

The answer to the longing in Hudson Taylor's heart was found in the counsel of a fellow missionary, John McCarthy, who wrote:

"To let my loving Savior work in me His will, my sanctification is what I would live for by His grace. Abiding, not striving nor struggling; looking off unto Him; trusting Him for present power; trusting Him to subdue all inward corruption; resting in the love of an almighty Savior, in the conscious joy of a complete salvation, a salvation 'from all sin' (this is His Word); willing that His will should truly be supreme – this is not new, and yet 'tis new to me. I feel as though the first dawning of a glorious day had risen upon me. I hail it with trembling, yet with trust. I seem to have got to the edge only, but of a sea which is boundless; to have sipped only, but of that which fully satisfies. Christ literally all seems to me now the power, the only

power for service; the only ground for unchang-
ing joy. May He lead us into the realization of His
unfathomable fullness." [25]

The "realization of His unfathomable fullness" is part of
the experience Paul described as Christ increasingly living His life through our yielded lives (Gal.2:20). It is living moment by moment of each day completely sustained
by the life of Christ in us. It is the incessant yielding of our
lives to the control of the Spirit of Christ dwelling within.
Then the life we live is "not striving or struggling," but
rather simply abiding in the overcoming, victorious life
of Jesus within.

The Apostle Peter described it this way: "If anyone
serves, he should do it with the strength God provides,
so that in all things God may be praised through Jesus
Christ. To him be the glory and the power for ever and
ever" (1 Peter 4:11).

Service to others done merely through an altruistic
spirit may be helpful and commendable. The result is
that good things are done and people may be helped by
me. However, when my service is fueled by God's powerful, undeserved activity in my life, then the result is that
great things are done and people are helped by God …
and ultimately He is glorified.

Take Away for Today: I challenge you this week to live a life sustained by the grace of God. Let His powerful, undeserved activity fuel all you do ... and watch the supernatural unfold before your eyes.

Part IV ~ Day 3
Unwrapping Your Spiritual Gifts

Today's Scripture Reading: I Corinthians 12:1-13

In his book *The Holy Spirit: The Key to Supernatural Living*, Dr. Bill Bright tells the story of a West Texas sheep rancher by the name of Ira Yates. The Great Depression of the 1930s hit Yates particularly hard. Because he wasn't able to make enough on his ranching operation to pay the principal and interest on the mortgage, he was in danger of losing his ranch. With little money for clothes or food, his family (like many others) had to live on government subsidy. Day after day, as he grazed his sheep over barren West Texas country, he worried about how he would pay his bills. Then one day a seismographic crew from an oil company came into the area and told him there might be oil on his land. They asked permission to drill a wildcat well, Yates signed a lease contract, and they struck a huge oil reserve. The first well came in at 80,000 barrels a day. Many subsequent wells were more than twice as large. In fact, what would later become known as the Yates Oil Field was one of the largest in the country at the time. And Mr.

Yates owned it all. The day he purchased the land he had received the oil and mineral rights. Yet, he'd been living on welfare. Imagine that … a multimillionaire living in poverty. What was the problem? He didn't know the oil was there even though he owned it. [26]

Amazingly many believers are vastly ignorant of the incredible supernatural ability deposited in them for effective service. They are not aware of the vast reservoir of power that resides in them by the Holy Spirit, and is available to them in service of the King. For this reason the Apostle Paul wrote to the first century Corinthian church about this very issue: "Now about spiritual gifts, brothers, I do not want you to be ignorant" (1 Corinthians 12:1).

My purpose in this chapter is not to give a thorough or technical treatise on spiritual gifts, but rather to spark in you a desire to discover, develop and deploy your spiritual giftedness for the service and glory of God.

Believe it or not, when you come to discover and unwrap the unique spiritual gift that God has given you, it is one of the most exhilarating and fulfilling things that can happen in your life. It will open up new realms of effectiveness and meaning in your life of service.

Numerous definitions of spiritual gifts have been given. Kenneth Hemphill says that "spiritual gifts are graciously given by God to enable believers to participate fully in the edification of the church and the advance of the kingdom (of God)." [27] William McRae says that a spiritual gift "is a divine endowment of a special ability for service upon a member of the body of Christ." [28]

C. Peter Wagner defines a spiritual gift as "a special attribute given by the Holy Spirit to every member of the Body of Christ according to God's grace for use within the context of the Body."[29] You will recognize parts of each of these definitions in the biblical explanations that follow.

SPIRITUAL GIFTS ARE GIVEN THROUGH THE HOLY SPIRIT

The moment you were saved God deposited His Spirit within you and you were born again. So God is dwelling in you by His Spirit to produce a remarkable life … a life of Christ-like, selfless service. You see, God didn't give you His Spirit just to make you *happy*. He did it to make you *holy* … and to make you *helpful* in His Kingdom. When the Holy Spirit comes to dwell within a believer He brings with Him unique abilities known as spiritual gifts. "Now to each one the manifestation of the Spirit is given for the common good" (1 Corinthians 12:7).

SPIRITUAL GIFTS ARE GIVEN BY GRACE.

The Bible says that "there are different kinds of gifts, but the same Spirit" (1 Corinthians 12:4). The word for "gift" here literally means "grace gift." It all begins with the grace of God. "We have different gifts, according to the grace given us" (Romans 12:6a). A spiritual gift is not an *adornment*, but an *anointing* by the Holy Spirit. They are handed down, not worked up. "But to each one of us grace has been given as Christ apportioned it" (Ephesians 4:7). Because they are given by grace, we may take no credit for the possession or benefits from spiritual gifts. The Spirit determines who gets what gifts (v.11), so no one can think they have been marked out for special status because of their gifts. Some of the gifts are more visible than others, but none is more essential than the others.

In two different places the Apostle Paul says that there are different kinds of gifts (1 Corinthians 12:4; Romans 12:6). This points to the fact that there are a number of distinct spiritual gifts given to believers. Bible scholars do not agree on the exact number and distinction of kinds of gifts. Catalogues of spiritual gifts and/or gifted persons are found in Romans 12:3-8; I Corinthians 12:4-11,27-30; Ephesians 4:7-13; and I Peter 4: 8-11. Because these Scriptural lists are not identical, it seems clear that God did not intend to give His church either a rigid or a precise and exhaustive list of gifts, but rather general categories.

SPIRITUAL GIFTS ARE GIVEN FOR SERVICE.

"There are different kinds of service, but the same Lord"

(1 Corinthians 12:5). The word "service" means a ministry; the word is the word from which we get our word "deacon." Yet service is not limited to those who have the church office of deacon. God gives each of us spiritual gifts which are used in a variety of different ministries.

Spiritual gifts are activated for service to God in and through the church. "Each one should use whatever gift he has received to serve others, faithfully administering God's grace in its various forms" (1 Peter 4:10). We must never forget that the gifts are for loving ministry in the church. They are not for our own gratification. They are for church edification. When this is ignored, confusion sets in.

THE SPIRITUAL GIFTS ARE GIVEN WITH POWER.

The spiritual gifts are a result of God's powerful working in a person's life, and they result in God powerfully working through us in the lives of other people. "There are different kinds of working, but the same God works all of them in all men" (1 Corinthians 12:6). The word "working" means "effects" or "energy." God provides the spiritual gifts and the power and faith with which to exercise those gifts. They are given supernaturally and energized supernaturally.

SPIRITUAL GIFTS ARE GIVEN TO EVERY BELIEVER.

"Now to each one the manifestation of the Spirit is given for the common good" (1 Corinthians 12:7). The spiritual gifts differ from natural talents. Gifts have a spiritual explanation; talents have a natural explanation. Another way to describe spiritual gifts is that they are a "manifestation of the Spirit." They reveal the Holy Spirit of Almighty God whenever those gifts operate. They are not hidden; they are manifest (evident). God wants your gift to work! That kind of manifestation is given to *every* believer.

All believers have at least one spiritual gift, but no one believer possesses all of the gifts. Every believer is to use their gift in at least one ministry. That ministry is to be the place where that gift becomes the outflow of God's power into the lives of other people.

I vividly remember when, as a college student, I awakened to this reality. God had done a great work in my life and I was growing in my walk with Christ. One evening I drove to a nearby town to hear some friends who sang in a Christian singing group. As I sat through the concert and listened as my friends ministered I found myself feeling jealous that I didn't have a talent I could use in ministry. Those feelings carried over to my hour-long drive back home. I asked the Lord if there was anything He could do through me. I vividly remember my car suddenly filling with a sense of God's presence. In no uncertain terms the Lord assured me that if I made myself completely available to Him He would use me in ministering to others. My gifts and abilities were different from those of my friends, but God had ways that He wanted to use me. That was a real breakthrough for me. Before long I was given opportunities to lead Bible studies on my college campus. Soon a church contacted me about serving as a part-time student minister. Having been a pastor now for many years I still look back on that evening as a turning point in my life.

Brad Waggoner puts it this way: "Your gifts have been given to you as part of God's unique creative work in you, and identifying the gifts you have been entrusted with is a key step toward discovering God's unique plan for your life. When a Christian discovers His kingdom mission, a mission of service no one else can fulfill, it changes his entire life." [30]

Take Away for Today: You may be looking at your life and wondering if you are destined to simply sit on the sidelines of service to the Lord while others actually get in the game. If you will make yourself available to the Lord, He will show you when, where and how you are to use the gifts for ministry He has given you.

PART IV ~ DAY 4
GETTING AN M.B.A

Today's Scripture Reading: John 13:1-16

Some years ago the legendary football coach and commentator Bud Wilkinson was asked to serve on the President's Council for Physical Fitness. On one occasion he was being interviewed and a reporter asked him what contribution professional football made to the physical fitness of Americans. To the surprise of everyone listening Wilkinson said, "Very little! A professional football game is a happening where 50,000 spectators desperately needing exercise, sit in the stands watching 22 men on the field desperately needing rest."

Ironically that sounds like the typical church. Estimates are that in the average church today 80% of the service is done by 20% of the members. That would not, however, be the case if every believer knew how to unwrap their spiritual gift and put it to use in meaningful service in their church and community.

Jesus constantly battled the worldly mindset of His followers. They tended to look at life the way their pagan neighbors did. Important people have many people serve them. Jesus turned that mentality upside down: "Not so with you. Instead, whoever wants to become great among you must be your servant, and whoever wants to be first must be slave of all" (Mark 10:43). According to Jesus greatness is not measured by how many people *serve you*, but by how many *you serve*. Self-centered people think, "*Serve us!*" Christ-followers think, "*Service.*"

Somewhere I heard about a company that only employed persons with an M.B.A. Thinking it stood for a Masters of Business Administration it seemed a little strange that a company would require *every* person in the company to have such an advanced business degree. Why would that be necessary for an engineer or a facilities manager or a data entry person? It all made sense to me when I discovered that the M.B.A. required by the company was not a "Master of Business Administration" but rather a "Mop Bucket Attitude." This was the company's way of saying they were seeking after employees, no matter what their position was, who didn't think it was beneath them to grab a mop to clean up a spill in the office. That kind of selflessness is valuable in the secular world as well as in the church.

Earlier we were reminded of how on the night before Jesus was crucified He gathered His disciples in a borrowed room. As they all gathered from the dusty Jerusalem streets everyone knew that someone would have the lowly duty of washing the feet of the others. Then Jesus surprised them by taking up a towel and a basin of water and began to go around the room washing the feet of His disciples. It was a calculated action on Jesus' part; his followers needed this lesson in the true measure of greatness: "Now that I, your Lord and Teacher, have washed your feet, you also should wash one another's feet" (John 13:14).

The point I want to make here is that the service of Jesus was very practical, even routine. That's the beauty of this kind of servant's attitude. Richard Foster observes that "radical self-denial gives the feel of adventure. If we forsake all, we even have the chance of glorious martyrdom. But in service we are banished to the mundane, the ordinary, the trivial." [31] So this servant's attitude is for the glory of God and the practical good of others ... period.

It is this kind of service that is to exemplify every Christ-follower in every church. The Apostle Paul wrote to the church in Philippi about this very issue: "Make my joy complete by being like-minded, having the same love, being one in spirit and purpose. Do nothing out of selfish ambition or vain conceit, but in humility consider others better than yourselves. Each of you should look not only to your own interests, but also to the interests of others" (Philippians 2:2-4).

Think of how much goes on in our churches and in our homes that is characterized by selfish ambition, vain conceit, and looking only to our own interests. We might never admit it, but deep inside we pridefully assume that our comfort, convenience, preferences and needs are really more important than anyone else's. Why else would be behave in such selfish ways?

The truth of God's Word calls us away from that attitude and into a life of putting others first ... the essence of a "Mop Bucket Attitude." But what does this look like? Richard Foster, in his book *Celebration of Discipline*, describes service as a spiritual discipline ... a means of training ourselves for godliness. He lists a number of ways that service can take shape in the marketplace of our lives:

- *The service of hiddenness.* When we are content to serve in ways that are not readily noticed by others it is a rebuke to our flesh and to pride. Surprisingly, there is actually great joy in doing something that goes unnoticed by others.

- *The service of small things.* Many of the Christ-motivated acts of service are found in the "tiny insignificant corners of life" where we assist others. Jesus' actions forged great meaning into the smallest of serving deeds.

- *The service of guarding the reputation of others.* When we know a shortcoming in the life of another and hold our tongue about it this strengthens the virtue of humility in us. To guard the reputation of another guards our own hearts against pride and arrogance.

- *The service of being served.* When Jesus washed the feet of the disciples Peter actually refused. On the surface that sounds like humility; in reality it was an act of veiled pride. Sometimes it is humbling to allow ourselves to be served by another. It causes us to accept the fact that we need others.

- *The service of common courtesy.* Showing common courtesy to others acknowledges and affirms the worth of others.

- *The service of hospitality.* We have lost this virtue in contemporary times, but it was a big deal in biblical times. Opening our home to others demonstrates that our life, our time, our privacy and our belongings are not our own.

- *The service of listening.* There is probably no more practical way of demonstrating love to another than by simply listening to them. This requires us to set aside our desire to talk, and our desire to be heard, in order to serve another.

- *The service of bearing the burdens of others.* Foster says that love is most perfectly fulfilled when we bear the hurts and sufferings of each other.

- *The service of sharing the Word of Life.* We are dependent upon one another for the necessary wisdom of life. When we share the wisdom of the Spirit and Scripture with one another we perform a valuable service.[32]

The Apostle Paul exhorted the leaders of the church in Ephesus to follow his example of selfless service: "In everything I did, I showed you that by this kind of hard work we must help the weak, remembering the words the Lord Jesus himself said: 'It is more blessed to give than to receive'" (Acts 20:35).

Take Away for Today: Do you really believe Jesus' words are true ... that it is more blessed to give than receive. I challenge you to pour your life into serving God and others today. Be blessed!

PART IV ~ DAY 5
GREAT IS YOUR REWARD

Today's Scripture Reading: Matthew 25:14-30

Our supreme motivation in serving God and others is the glory of God and His Son. Knowing that, it may confuse us when we learn that the Bible actually says a great deal about rewards for serving. We have learned that it is more blessed to give than to receive (Acts 20:35). So there is a blessing involved, but it's much greater than you may imagine.

In Jesus' Sermon on the Mount He cautioned His followers about doing righteous acts of service (like giving to the needy) in order to be seen by others. "If you do, *you will have no reward* from your Father in heaven" (Matthew 6:1b, italics mine). Jesus went on to give instructions as to how to appropriately give to the needy without drawing attention to the deed. "Then your Father, who sees what is done in secret, *will reward you*" (Matthew 6:4b, italics mine). So there is the worthwhile anticipation of future rewards.

I love reading the biographies of the presidents of the United States. A few years ago one of my daughters gave me a copy of the biography of Theodore Roosevelt entitled *Colonel Roosevelt* by Edmund Morris. Actually this is the third volume in a three-part biography of one of the most colorful characters in US and world history.

Colonel Roosevelt picks up with Roosevelt on the African safari he commenced shortly after he completed his second term in the White House. He was met with great throngs of admirers along every stop in Africa. At the conclusion of the safari Roosevelt and his family spent three months travelling throughout Europe, again, greeted with tremendous fanfare everywhere they stopped.

Then came his long-anticipated return to the United States. Hopes were high that Roosevelt would run for a third term as president; many Americans clamored for more of this larger-than-life individual. When his ship sailed into the harbor in New York City tens of thousands of people awaited him. As he disembarked from his ship Roosevelt was greeted by dignitaries from every branch of government, as well as people from every walk of life.

As I came to this part of Roosevelt's story I was reminded of a story I heard years ago of something that happened to some other passengers on Roosevelt's ship that day. This unnamed husband and wife were retiring missionaries, returning home after years of selfless service in Africa, where Roosevelt had been hunting for the better part of a year. As they disembarked they saw the spectacle of the crowds awaiting the president. They heard a band playing in the background. Yet, for the returning missionary couple there was no receiving party; in fact, not one person was there to meet them. Discouraged, the husband sadly groaned, "I didn't want a parade, but at least someone could have come to welcome us home!" With that his wise wife turned to him and replied, "Honey, we are not home yet."

It's important to keep our lives in perspective. This world is not our home; and neither will we receive our applause from this world. The Apostle Paul understood this: "On the contrary, we speak as men approved by God to be entrusted with the gospel. We are not trying to please men but God, who tests our hearts" (1 Thessalonians 2:4).

Richard Foster says that, "True service rests contented in hiddenness. It does not fear the lights and blare of attention, but it does not seek them either … the divine nod of approval is completely sufficient." [33]

Live each day with eternity in mind. Live for the applause of heaven, not for the applause of this world. One day all God's faithful servants will be welcomed home; their reward will be great. To illustrate this Jesus told a parable about man who went on a journey (Matthew 25:14-30). While he was away he entrusted various amounts of money to three different servants. Two of the three invested the money given them by the master. The third man hid the small amount that was entrusted to him. When the master returned he demanded an accounting from his servants. The two servants who had invested their master's money revealed the profit they had earned for their master. The third servant was faced with having to explain to his master why he had done nothing with the master's money to earn a dividend. The third servant was severely chastised and punished for his lack of diligence. The two faithful stewards were commended by their master: "Well done, good and faithful servant! You have been faithful with a few things; I will put you in charge of many things. Come and share your master's happiness!" (Matthew 25:21).

While the Bible has a good deal to say about rewards for the righteous, we might wish for a few more details about exactly how we will be rewarded when we stand before our Master and Lord in heaven. I have heard many ill-informed attempts at explaining the rewards God has for the faithful. Many of them are merely extensions of our materialistic dreams on the earth ... magnificent mansions, streets of gold, pearly gates, grand family reunions, even plush golf courses. Certainly there is biblical justification for expecting that heaven will be the full completion of all that earth is lacking in the way of security and provision, but is that really our reward? I get the impression that many Christians are looking forward to going to heaven *whether God is there or not.*

The life God envisions for us begins here on this earth when we are saved; it culminates in a glorious way in our life in the new heaven and the new earth. Remember that this life is none other than the very life of God manifested through His Son Jesus Christ. The amazing thing about our heavenly reward is that it is all about God!

Notice how Peter describes our inheritance to suffering believers: "Praise be to the God and Father of our Lord Jesus Christ! In his great mercy he has given us new birth into a living hope through the resurrection of Jesus Christ from the dead, and into an inheritance that can never perish, spoil or fade—kept in heaven for you" (1 Peter 1:3). Notice that our inheritance is not heaven ... it is kept *in* heaven.

Whatever our rewards may look like, the great thing about them is their connection to the life God has envisioned for us. Our reward in heaven is Him! In the parable Jesus told the master said, "Come and share your master's happiness." That's our reward ... we get to share in our Master's joy, which is His own glory.

As a pastor I have officiated at countless funerals through the years. In most funerals there is a time to eulogize (praise) the individual who is being remembered. Usually I, or a friend or family member of the deceased, will recount the person's accomplishments, or how they endeared themselves to others. Inevitably, during times like that, I find myself wondering: "How will others remember me when I'm gone? Will my service to God and to others be foremost in everyone's thinking as they recollect my life?" For sure this can't be motivated by a hunger for notoriety, but simply by the desire to be found faithful to Jesus in "doing good" as long as we have breath in our bodies.

Take Away for Today: As you go through today, conduct an "audit" of your life. What percentage of your day is being spent serving God and others? Notice in your work, in your interactions with others, even in your recreation, ways that you can selflessly serve God by loving others.

PART V
ENVISION ... SHARING
JESUS CHRIST

ENVISION: You have a clear understanding of the gospel of Jesus Christ. You clearly communicate the message in the power of the Holy Spirit in the course of everyday life. You regularly cross cultural and geographical barriers to develop relationships with people far from God. You help others respond to God's love and to follow Jesus Christ. You possess a biblical worldview which energizes you as a Christian citizen to impact your culture. You consistently look for openings to begin a spiritual conversation with others. You look for ways to broaden your circle of relationships to include people who need to know Christ. You pray regularly for non-believers in your circle of influence, asking God to show them their need for Christ. You hunger to be part of God's grand quest to take the gospel to the nations, and are continuously open to how He might include you in that quest.

SCRIPTURAL FOUNDATION: Matthew 4:19; 5:14-16; 9:37-38; Matthew 28:18-20; John 4:35-37; Acts 1:8; Romans 10:14-17; II Corinthians 5:18-21; I Peter 3:15-16

PART V ~ DAY 1
GOD'S GLORIOUS QUEST

Today's Scripture Reading: II Corinthians 5:11-21

To this day I remember my first attempt at sharing my faith with another person. I worked for a moving company in the summer after my freshman year in college. Although I had been a believer since my early teenage years, I had never attempted to even invite someone to church, much less share the gospel with them. But that year God had done a great work in my life and as result I found myself more motivated to talk to others about Jesus.

One of my coworkers was also a college student and I began to have a burden to speak to him about Christ … but I didn't even know where to start. So I began to pray that God would open a door for me to talk to my coworker about his relationship with the Lord. One day I needed a ride home from work and I asked my coworker if he could give me a lift. He was glad to do it, and on the drive home he shocked me by asking a question: "Mike, I've noticed something different about you in the last few months. What's up?" I knew that there was something different in my relationship with the Lord, but I had no idea it was showing. So I took a deep breath and shared about my journey of following Jesus, including how God had recently jolted me into a deeper relationship with Himself. My friend accepted my invitation to attend church with me the next week. I do not know if my friend ever put his trust in Christ for the gift of eternal life; I only know it was a real breakthrough for me to know that God could use me to introduce others to Himself.

Of all the attributes of a Christ-follower nothing is more intimidating to most of us than the task of sharing Jesus Christ with others. Perhaps it is the fear of failure; no one wants to mess up when another person's eternal destiny is at stake. Or perhaps it is the fear of rejection; we feel that rejection of the gospel is a rejection of us personally. Or perhaps it is sheer selfish pride; we just don't want bad people to have what we have as believers. Or, most sadly, we have little interest in the spiritual condition of the people around us.

These are all very self-centered reasons/excuses for not sharing Christ with others. For us to be able to break through all of that we must be overwhelmed by the grand life-giving vision of God in the task of evangelism as it is revealed in the gospel. I'm convinced that our greatest challenge in this endeavor is to understand the amazing mission God commenced when He sent His Son to this world to die for our sins.

The Apostle Paul describes it in these terms: "All this is from God, who reconciled us to himself through Christ and gave us the ministry of reconciliation: that God was reconciling the world to himself in Christ, not counting men's sins against them. And he has committed to us the message of reconciliation. We are therefore Christ's ambassadors, as though God were making his appeal through us. We implore you on Christ's behalf: Be reconciled to God (II Corinthians 5:18 -20).

I aim to remind you of the reality of something that is going on all around us that we are often blind to – to what God is doing all around you every day – something He is doing in the life of every person you see. This means the person in the car next to you on the freeway, in the aisle at Wal-Mart, in the hallway at school. This means the person whose lifestyle is utterly repulsive to you. I aim to alert you to something that God is doing this very moment, not just where you live, but in the jungles of Africa, in the mega-cities of India, and in the villages of Great Britain. What is this reality? It is that God is actively working to reconcile His enemies to Himself. Furthermore, He wants to do it through Christ-followers.

What was God doing in sending His Son Jesus Christ into the world? He was reconciling us to Himself. Notice that He was not reconciling Himself to us, but us to Himself. In love He created us in His own image and for His own purposes. But we rebelled against Him and His laws through our sin. Infected with the disease of sin (our sin nature) we are dead spiritually, and deserve to be separated from God for eternity (the essence of death). In spite of God's love for us, our sin placed us in direct opposition to a holy God. By virtue of this we are objects of God's holy displeasure against sin (wrath). Here's how the New Testament describes our condition apart from Christ: "As for you, you were dead in your transgressions and sins, in which you used to live when you followed the ways of this world and of the ruler of the kingdom of the air, the spirit who is now at work in those who are disobedient. All of us also lived among them at one time, gratifying the cravings of our sinful nature and following its desires and thoughts. Like the rest, we were by nature objects of wrath" (Ephesians 2:1-3).

Then God in His glorious grace did something amazing. "When we were God's enemies, we were reconciled to him through the death of his Son..." (Romans 5:10a). Or to put it in different terms: "But because of his great love for us, God, who is rich in mercy, made us alive with Christ even when we were dead in transgressions—it is by grace you have been saved" (Ephesians 2:4-5).

God "reconciled the world to himself in Christ, not counting men's sins against them," (II Corinthians 5:19a). How could this be? Did God simply ignore our sin? No! Did we somehow do enough good deeds to atone for our own sin? Absolutely not! Then how was it that our sins were not counted against us? They were counted against *Christ*. As he hung upon that Roman instrument of capital punishment (the cross) God heaped our sins on Christ. So when by faith and repentance we cry out to God for rescue, our guilt is imputed to Christ ... and His righteousness is credited to us. "God made him who had no sin to be sin for us, so that in him we might become the righteousness of God" (2 Corinthians 5:21).

Our efforts in sharing Jesus Christ must start at this point. God was on a grand, glorious, gracious mission to reconcile the world to Himself. If, as you read these words, you have been saved, you are in that condition solely because God came to you on a merciful quest to reconcile you to Himself.

The task of witnessing sheds most its fears, reservations and frustrations when we understand that we are on mission with God. It all started with God seeing our helpless, hopeless condition and coming to our rescue in the Person of His Son and our Savior. He secured our redemption by paying the price for our sin by the sacrificial, atoning sacrifice of His Son on the cross of Calvary. Knowing that we, in the deadness of our sin, are incapable of responding to Him, graciously He made us "response-able." He effectually called us to Himself and sent His Holy Spirit to effect the new birth in us. Glory to His Name!

If our efforts to share Jesus Christ with others start at any other point, or on any other basis, those efforts are ill-motivated and ill-conceived. The bringing about of the life God envisions for us through Christ is solely for His glory. In His grace God chose to include us in the breath-taking adventure of delivering the Good News to perishing souls. Whenever and however we go about that, it must be for His glory.

Take Away for Today: Try living every moment of this day in the awe of what God did for you in sending His Son to die for your sins. Consciously rejoice in the fact that God came into this world in the person of His Son Jesus on a grand mission … to reconcile you to Himself.

PART V ~ DAY 2
PARTNERS WITH GOD

Today's Scripture Reading: Romans 10:14-21

For many believers the task of sharing Jesus Christ with others is a burdensome task. Will Metzger in his helpful book on evangelism entitled *Tell the Truth* says, "Nothing has the potential of producing more guilt among Christian than this subject (unless it's sex!)."[34] Let's face it, many of us feel about the work of evangelism the way we might feel about climbing Mt. Everest. It would be great if we could do it successfully, but it's just way beyond our ability. This is the case because we do not understand how God has included us in His glorious quest.

I thought about this one night when our family was having a game night. We happen to be playing Nintendo's bowling game because it's something that just about everyone can do, except for our little granddaughter Caroline, who was three years old at the time. She couldn't quite get the trigger thing yet, but we let her participate. I gave her a controller that didn't work, and when it was my turn to bowl, I told her she could bowl for me. So she would stand by the TV and act like she was bowling. However, what was actually happening was that I was standing behind her with the real controller that made the game work. So I would roll the ball, and if I got a strike, Caroline thought she was getting the strike. She would jump up and down with joy. She thought she was really getting the hang of it. Every time it was her turn to bowl she just jumped up with great confidence and slung her arm and the ball would roll down the lane and she was always happy with the results. On one of the frames of bowling her daddy took his turn and when he didn't get a strike or a spare he said "Aw, I missed it" or something like that. Well confident little Caroline turned to her dad and said, "Dad, do you want me to help you with that?"

You see, she didn't understand what was really happening in the game. She thought she was doing something really great, when it was actually someone else who was doing something great. Before long she thought she was the expert.

In evangelism we are partners with God, and not just in a pretend sort of way (like giving my granddaughter a controller that didn't work). We have something very significant to bring to the process, and God in His grace chooses to use us. Remember: "All this is from God, who reconciled us to himself through Christ and *gave us the ministry of reconciliation*: that God was reconciling the world to himself in Christ, not counting men's sins against them. And *he has committed to us the message of reconciliation.* We are therefore Christ's ambassadors, *as though God were making his appeal through us.* We implore you on Christ's behalf: Be reconciled to God" (2 Corinthians 5:18-20, italics mine).

There are many facets to our involvement with God in reconciling people to Him, but here the Apostle Paul underscores the primary one. This "ministry of reconciliation" that has been given to us involves a message that is to be proclaimed (the gospel). God is making an appeal (speaking) through us. There's a chain of events that occurs whenever a person calls on the name of the Lord to be saved: "How, then, can they call on the one they have not believed in? And how can they believe in the one of whom they have not heard? And how can they hear without someone preaching to them? And how can they preach unless they are sent? As it is written, 'How beautiful are the feet of those who bring good news!' ... Consequently, faith comes from hearing the message, and the message is heard through the word of Christ" (Romans 10:14-15, 17).

The biblical pattern for personal evangelism always involves a verbal witness in the sharing of the gospel of Jesus Christ. (In a later chapter I'll talk how we build bridges into the lives of others for the purpose of communicating the Good News.) It is imperative that we carefully study the basic tenets of the gospel so that we can clearly and accurately communicate it to others. "I am not ashamed of the gospel, because it is the power of God for the salvation of everyone who believes: first for the Jew, then for the Gentile. For in the gospel a righteousness from God is revealed, a righteousness that is by faith from first to last, just as it is written: 'The righteous will live by faith'" (Romans 1:16-17). If we fail to communicate the whole gospel we are in danger of giving a non-believer a placebo that has no power to actually save them.

Yes, the stakes are high; but it isn't all on our shoulders. It is God who saves the lost, no matter how effective or ineffective our efforts. But the fact still remains that God, in His grace, chooses to use us in bringing precious souls into His glorious Kingdom.

The life God envisions for us includes sharing Jesus Christ with others in a clear and compelling way. This assignment, along with the power to do it, comes with the package of eternal life. When Jesus called His first disciples He said, "Follow me and I will make you fishers of men" (Matthew 4:19). Just think of all that Jesus could have said there: "Follow me and I will make you ... great husbands ... terrific moms ... faithful money managers ... skilled Bible scholars." All of those are certainly desirable traits, but that's not what Jesus promised to do. As a follower of Jesus one of the first things He will teach us to do is to fish for people. Later Jesus promised the help of the Holy Spirit: "You will receive power when the Holy Spirit comes on you; *and you will be my witnesses ...*" (Acts 1:8a, italics mine). The power that comes upon us by the Holy

Spirit at our conversion is for the purpose bold proclamation of the gospel of Jesus Christ.

As a student at Southwestern Baptist Theological Seminary in the 1970s I had the privilege of studying under Dr. Oscar Thompson, a distinguished pastor and evangelism professor. He wrote a book entitled *Concentric Circles of Concern* in which he asserted that the gospel moves most effectively "on contiguous lines – along lines of relationships." [35]

God sovereignly works in our lives to place us in contact with people with whom He wants us to share the gospel of Christ. God has placed you in a circle of relationships. They include your family, your friends, your neighbors, your classmates and coworkers. Yet there are more people in your circle than you may realize. Your circle also includes the people you encounter each day at the cleaners, at the coffee shop, at the doctor's office or at the gym. Every time your traffic pattern changes it brings different people into your circle.

Research has proven that people are much more likely to attend church if they are invited by a loved one or friend. That's an interesting statistic in light of the fact that churches generally don't capitalize on that approach. We spend extraordinary amounts of money on advertising and other efforts to get our message out to the community, all the while we ignore that advertising that is priceless ... the simple invitation by a family member or friend.

Granted, attending church is not synonymous with being saved, but it is most often the first step that people take toward Christ. The New Testament tells of simple invitation offered by a man named Philip to his friend Nathanael. It is pointed and powerful … "Come and see" (John 1:45-46).

I'm praying that God will open your eyes, your heart and your arms to the people in the circle where He has placed you. You are not there by accident. God has placed you there. You may chafe at the fact that there are some people in your circle whom you do not like. Maybe their lifestyle is repulsive to you. Maybe they are so different from you that you really don't think you have a thing in the world in common with them. Maybe you're just ambivalent towards them, or you just outright despise them. Yet there they are in your circle. If you believe that God is sovereign in all the matters of your life, then you have to believe that God has orchestrated your life in such a way as to bring them to you for what He wants to do through you to touch them. It's no accident that they are in your circle.

Take Away for Today: Yield yourself to God. Confess to Him your fears and inhibitions about sharing Christ with others. As you go through the day make a mental note of the people you encounter in the circle of your life and what their spiritual condition might be.

PART V ~ DAY 3
WITH GREAT BOLDNESS

Today's Scripture Reading: Acts 4:23-31

The word "bold" might be the last word you would use to describe your witness. Perhaps it will encourage you to know that even the mighty apostles who had first-hand knowledge of Jesus, and who were eye-witnesses to the reality of the resurrection, still needed to pray for boldness in their witnessing.

The setting is Jerusalem. The two leading apostles, Peter and John, were dragged before the Jewish leaders and questioned about their involvement in the healing of a crippled beggar (see Acts 3). Even in the face of persistent grilling Peter and John maintained their composure and their wits. They spoke the gospel in a clear and compelling way. The authorities were amazed: "When they saw the courage of Peter and John and realized that they were unschooled, ordinary men, they were astonished and they took note that these men had been with Jesus" (Acts 4:13). There was something about the way these ordinary men handled themselves in front of a hos-

181

tile audience. Even the people who were responsible for the crucifixion of Jesus recognized that these men were different because they had been with Jesus.

Before releasing Peter and John the authorities warned that they should speak no more in the name of this Jesus. Once again with great courage they replied, "For we cannot help speaking about what we have seen and heard" (Acts 4:20). Having been threatened, Peter and John returned to the gathering place of the church where they reported all that had happened to them. Immediately the band of believers began to pray with great fervor, raising their voices in prayer to God. Their praying builds and builds toward this huge request: "Now, Lord, consider their threats and enable your servants to speak your word with great boldness" (Acts 4:29).

I'm amazed at their audacity. Notice some important words in this prayer:

"Now, Lord..." This all starts with the understanding that God is Lord, as is His Son Jesus Christ. We are men and women under authority. We are not free to live our lives according to our own wishes. He is Lord and we are to obey Him.

"Consider their threats..." They knew they could trust God to take care of whatever opposition they experienced. Jesus Himself endured and overcame resistance to His message. Their risen Lord knew what His witnesses were facing and would give them courage to face the opposition. This should encourage believers in places around the world where bold witnessing like this means certain jail time, beatings, and sometimes worse.

"Enable your servants..." They understood their roles as servants of the Lord. The word for "servants" actually means "slaves." The Lord Jesus is our Master, but He is not an abusive one. We may serve Him with complete abandon knowing that He loves us.

"Enable your servants to speak your word..." They understood their own weaknesses and the necessity for God to give them something that didn't come naturally to them ... the power for effective witness. In Acts 1:8 Jesus promised that we will receive power when the Holy Spirit comes upon us and we will be His witnesses. The enabling power of the Holy Spirit comes upon God's obedient servants in response to our praying.

"Speak your word..." This is the assignment they were given. They were to speak God's word. The word for "speak" is not the word that is usually translated "preach" or "proclaim." It's the word for common speech. It's not just preaching the gospel from the pulpit; it is gossiping the gospel in everyday life. And note this: They were asking God to enable them to do the very thing that got them into hot water to begin with.

"With great boldness…" They were asking for boldness because they understood their natural tendency to not be bold in their witness. Timidity is like gravity that holds us down and holds us back. We need boldness to break the grip of our fears and to become courageous witnesses.

So what was the church most concerned about … what did they ask God for? Comfort or convenience? No, they were consumed with the passion to get the Word of God out to others. They asked for divine enabling, not escape; and God gave them the power that they needed.

The results were amazing and immediate: "After they prayed, the place where they were meeting was shaken. And they were all filled with the Holy Spirit and spoke the word of God boldly" (Acts 4:31). The prayer went up, the power came down, and the Word went forth.

The fire of the life we have in Christ will be evident in the flame of our evangelistic witness. Could it be that the reason we are not bolder in our witnessing is that Christ is not really that significant to us. Our zeal for Christ cannot be disconnected from our zeal in sharing Him with other people.

I'm always encouraged when I remember something that happened to a missionary from the 1800s, a man by the name of John Hyde, sometimes called Praying Hyde.

He was one of the first English speaking missionaries to go to India. One of his biographies tells of an experience he had on his voyage to India. Hyde opened an envelope containing a letter a friend gave him as he boarded the ship. His friend wrote to encourage Hyde to seek a fresh filling of the Holy Spirit before he entered the work in India. After reading the letter Hyde crumpled it up in anger and threw it on the deck of the ship. He resented that his friend implied that he was not fit for missionary service. But God used that letter in a powerful way. The Spirit of God was working in his heart. After a while he picked up the crumbled letter and read it again. Perhaps his friend was right. John Hyde would later write, "The result was that during the rest of that voyage I gave myself much to prayer that I might indeed be filled with the Holy Spirit." [36]

Take Away for Today: In your devotional time today, and each day, remember to ask God to open doors for you to share Christ with others. Expect that He will do that, and watch for how God works in this way. As God opens the doors, be courageous in your faith by walking through those doors into a relationship with a person who may be far from God.

PART V ~ DAY 4
STARTING SPIRITUAL CONVERSATIONS

Today's Scripture Reading: Acts 8:26-30

To some of His first followers Jesus said, "Come, follow me … and I will make you fishers of men" (Mark 1:17). The life Jesus envisioned for His followers clearly involved their being bold witnesses that attracted others to Christ. Jesus' call also indicates there is a training process involved. He would *make* them to be fishers of men. In essence Jesus intended to train His followers to be His partners in drawing persons to Himself.

Sometime back I bought a new coffee maker. On the outside of the box it showed several pictures: a piping hot cup of gourmet coffee, a cup of hot tea with a slice of lemon floating in it, a steaming cup of hot chocolate with marshmallows on top, and refreshing glasses of iced tea and iced coffee. Just under those pictures were the words, "All this and more at the touch of a button." So you might think that you could just take the coffee maker out of the box, push the button and instantly there was your cup of gourmet coffee. We all know, however, there's a lot more to it than that. You have to plug in the machine, and then fill the reservoir with water, and open the box of coffee packets, and insert one in the machine ... then at the touch of a button you're on your way to a great cup of coffee. So it's really not quite as simple as just touching the button.

As we think about the task of sharing Jesus Christ with other people, it's not just a matter of saying a few magic words and poof ... out comes a new Christian. It doesn't work that way. There's much work that goes into it from God's perspective and from ours.

I know for some of you this whole business of talking to others about Christ absolutely horrifies you. It will require a huge step of faith. You will have to depend on God like you've never had to depend on Him before. God is faithful. His grace is sufficient and His strength and power is perfected in our weaknesses. So if you feel really weak when it comes to this, there's room for God's power to work in and through you.

One of the greatest witnesses in the New Testament was a man named Philip. Acts 8 records a providential meeting that Philip had with an important official from Ethiopia. Let's tag along with Philip on his soul-winning visit to learn how to start and finish a spiritual conversation with people far from God.

"On that day a great persecution broke out against the church at Jerusalem, and all except the apostles were scattered throughout Judea and Samaria ... Those who were scattered preached the

word wherever they went." (Acts 8:1,4).

God wants to get us out of our holy huddles and out into the world where He will use us to communicate the truth to others. God often uses adverse circumstances to position us to where we will be His faithful witnesses. Do you wonder why your company transferred you to a position that you were not thrilled about taking? Do you wonder why you have to go for treatments at a cancer clinic every week? Has it occurred to you that God is using adversity to position you to be His witness to a new group of people?

"Now an angel of the Lord said to Philip, "Go south to the road—the desert road—that goes down from Jerusalem to Gaza" (Acts 8:26).

Again, this all starts with God. There are three persons involved in this event Philip, the Ethiopian official and the Lord ... but the Lord is the hero of the story. This all starts with God's heart of love for a lost man. Notice that Philip is not told at this point to whom He is to speak. He is simply told to "Go south." Historians tell us that there were actually two roads that go down from Jerusalem to Gaza. The "desert road," as it is called here, would have been the one less traveled. God sends Philip to a deserted place where you wouldn't think anything was happening. God, however, knows otherwise.

God doesn't necessarily deal with all of us the way He dealt with Philip. Sometimes God orchestrates things differently. He may redirect your path at the mall to where you suddenly encounter a friend you haven't seen in years. Why? Because God wants you to speak to them. Take those promptings from God seriously. You may not think the timing is all that great, but God knows the unique circumstances in the other person's life.

"So he started out, and on his way he met an Ethiopian eunuch, an important official in charge of all the treasury of Candace, queen of the Ethiopians. This man had gone to Jerusalem to worship, and on his way home was sitting in his chariot reading the book of Isaiah the prophet" (Acts 8:27-28).

Philip had no way of knowing that this particular man was already deep in thought about spiritual things. But God knew, and that's why He directed Philip to the road he was on. This was a divine appointment. What is apparent is that God is already at work in this Ethiopian man's life. He had gone all the way to Jerusalem to worship at the Temple there. He's either a Jew or at the very least a seeker of the God of the Jews. We also see he has in his possession a copy of the book of Isaiah. He has a Bible, and he's reading it. He's a seeker.

Now why would God pick out this solitary figure traveling cross-country? Only God knows? It is simply God's business at that moment to draw this man to Himself. We never know what God is doing and when or where He is going to do it. We simply must be sensitive.

In my first pastorate the chairman of our deacons was a man named Ellery Lawrence. One Saturday I had, of all things, gone to the dump grounds to haul off some trash. I stopped by the church on the way home. It was Saturday, and I didn't think anyone would be there to see (or smell) me in my dump clothing. It never fails when you think you'll never be seen, you'll be seen. Ellery drove up into the parking lot of the church in his pickup truck, came inside the church and said, "Pastor, I've had Jimmy and Wanda Jackson on my heart. Let's go over and witness to them." I was trying to think of a way of getting out of it. I was tired and sweaty. "Ellery, I'm not dressed to go visit anyone." Ellery persisted: "That's OK pastor, hop in my truck and let's go." So I did ... reluctantly. What happened in the next hour changed my whole attitude. We sat in the living room of this lumber yard worker and his wife and shared Jesus with then ... and they both were saved! The next Sunday, they came forward during the invitation time of our worship service making their decision public and requesting to be baptized.

Two weeks later Wanda called me tremendously distraught. "Pastor, there's been an accident down at the lumber yard and Jimmy's been killed. Can you come?" As I drove to Jimmy and Wanda's home I remember being grateful that Ellery Lawrence was sensitive to the leading of the Holy Spirit. Had we not gone that day, Jimmy would likely have spent eternity in hell. Only God knew the events that were about to unfold in Jimmy and Wanda's life. God put it on Ellery's heart to go ... with his reluctant pastor in tow. In matters like this God orchestrates everything. We must be sensitive and obedient.

There are people all around you in whose heart's God is working. God works to position you to connect with them.

"The Spirit told Philip, 'Go to that chariot and stay near it … Then Philip ran up to the chariot…" (Acts 8:29-30a).

Here again we see this all starts in the heart of God. The Holy Spirit is talking to Philip; and Philip is responsive to the leading of the Lord. The Spirit directs Philip to go and make a connection with the man riding in the chariot.

Now that Philip has made a connection with this traveler he won't stop there. He will engage the man in a conversation that will result in the Ethiopian man's life being changed. More about that in the next chapter.

Take Away for Today: In Bill Hybel's book, *Just Walk Across the Room*, he states: "One thing I've learned is that life's great moments evolve from simple acts of cooperation with God's mysterious promptings – nudges that always lean toward finding what's been lost and freeing what's been enslaved." [37] Today be open to the people that God places in your classroom, conference room or break room. Take that huge step to just walk across the room to invest in someone's life for eternity.

PART V ~ DAY 5
FINISHING SPIRITUAL
CONVERSATIONS

Today's Scripture Reading: Acts 8:31-40

Recently Nan and I were walking across the parking lot at a shopping mall when we were stopped by a young woman. She asked us for directions to a particular department store she had heard about. She was new to Fort Worth and didn't know her way around. Nan was able to tell her exactly how to get to the store. During the course of the conversation I could tell there was something troubling this young lady. I asked, "So you're new to Fort Worth? What brings you here?" She replied that her father and mother had recently passed away and she just wanted to start over someplace new. I introduced myself to her, and she teared up as she said, "My dad's name was Mike."

As we talked with the young lady it became apparent that she had been drinking and was somewhat intoxicated. She was troubled in more ways than one. Though she tried to walk away a couple of times I kept pulling her back with questions. My last question was, "Do you like to go to church?" She said, "Oh yes, I love Jesus and I went to church back home." We invited her to our church and learned that she lives near our church. She promised to visit us soon. As the young lady walked away my heart ached for her. Deep down in her soul she needed the life that only Jesus could bring to her.

I wish I could say that I'm always alert to such opportunities. Far too many times I'm so busy with my own agenda that I often miss those souls that Jesus brings across my path. So let's get back to Philip and his divine appointment with the Ethiopian official traveling from Jerusalem back to his home. Let's see what we can learn from him.

"Then Philip ran up to the chariot and heard the man reading Isaiah the prophet. 'Do you understand what you are reading?' Philip asked" (Acts 8:30).

Know this: You will never invest in a non-believer's life that God hasn't already invested in. You will never love someone whom God hasn't loved first. God is already working. The very fact that He has brought you into contact with a person is an indication that God is sovereignly reaching into this person's life. It always starts with God.

Philip knew how to get his foot in the door, so to speak, but that's a little difficult when the door is a car door (or a chariot door) and it's going down the road at a good clip. I can just see Philip. He's running alongside the chariot, huffing and puffing. The Ethiopian's reading his Bible. Or better yet, imagine they're driving down the freeway. This guy's got his Bible open on the steering wheel in front of him. Philip pulls alongside the Ethiopian's car, lowers his window and hollers out to him, "Hey, do you understand what you're reading?" The Ethiopian looks up from his reading and does a double take. Who is this stranger driving alongside? So he pulls over to the side of the road and invites Philip on board.

Philip does this so skillfully. He simply asks a question, "Do you understand what you're reading?" One common misconception about sharing Christ with others is that believers think they have to do all the talking. Actually, one of the greatest ways to demonstrate Christian love to a nonbeliever is to simply listen to them.

"'How can I,' he said, 'unless someone explains it to me?' So he invited Philip to come up and sit with him" (Acts 8:31).

As God's providence would have it, at that very moment the Ethiopian man was reading a portion of the Old Testament in which the prophet Isaiah was speaking about the coming of the Messiah (Isaiah 53). Philip knew exactly what was in that part of Scripture.

"The eunuch was reading this passage of Scripture: 'He was led like a sheep to the slaughter, and as a lamb before the shearer is silent, so he did not open his mouth. In his humiliation he was deprived of justice. Who can speak of his descendants? For his life was taken from the earth.'" (Acts 8:32-33).

The man is clearly puzzled by this.

"The eunuch asked Philip, 'Tell me, please, who is the proph-

et talking about, himself or someone else?'" (Acts 8:34).

Now here is where so many of us get off track. We're responsive and attentive, but for some reason when the opportunity comes to make the transition to a conversation about the gospel, we freeze up. I'm impressed that Philip was familiar enough with the Scriptures that he could answer the man's questions. We don't have to be Bible scholars to be effective witnesses, but it is vitally important that we have a good working knowledge of the Scriptures in order to answer basic questions from non-believers.

"Then Philip began with that very passage of Scripture and told him the good news about Jesus" (Acts 8:35).

This is the key skill in sharing Jesus Christ with others. No matter what else is involved, you must tell them the good news (gospel) about Jesus. If God gives you the opportunity to do this, don't shrink back. The power to save is in the message of the gospel. The message of the gospel is all about what Jesus Christ did on the cross. If we try to get some kind of decision from people without giving them that important information we are not doing New Testament evangelism.

Now apparently something huge happens between v.35 and v.36.

"As they traveled along the road, they came to some water and the eunuch said, 'Look, here is water. Why shouldn't I be baptized?' Philip said, 'If you believe with all your heart you may.'

The eunuch answered, 'I believe that Jesus Christ is the Son of God'" (Acts 8:36-37).

Part of the presentation of the gospel is the call for a person to believe, to put their faith and trust, in Christ. In this case, the man immediately confessed his faith in Christ. "I believe that Jesus Christ is the Son of God."

Someone has defined successful witnessing as "sharing Jesus Christ with others and leaving the results to God." I like that definition because it reminds us of our part in the process of faithfully proclaiming the gospel to non-believers. It also reminds us that only God can work regeneration in the heart of a non-believer. That's why we must leave the results to God. By this definition, Philip was a faithful and successful witness for Christ, no matter how the Ethiopian man responded.

The Ethiopian man puts his faith in Christ, and in doing so makes the most important decision of his life. However, the spiritual conversation doesn't end here. There is more important work for Philip to do with his new brother in Christ.

"And he gave orders to stop the chariot. Then both Philip and the eunuch went down into the water and Philip baptized him" (Acts 8:38).

Hardly a week goes by that we don't hear a news story about a baby being abandoned in a garbage dumpster or on the steps of a fire station. Those stories rip at our hearts. Sadly, however, it also happens spiritually when a person is led to Christ, but there's no follow-through with them. Every new Christian is a spiritual baby in need of follow-through. When you help a person come to Christ, you are responsible for them. They are your spiritual child, so to speak. Don't abandon a newborn.

One of the most important parts of follow-up for a new Christian is that they understand they should be baptized. Apparently Philip explained this immediately after the man confessed Christ. Baptism is the public confession of faith that is expected of all believers. The Ethiopian man was confessing his faith in Christ to Philip, but also to his entourage that was accompanying a man of such importance.

"When they came up out of the water, the Spirit of the Lord suddenly took Philip away, and the eunuch did not see him again, but went on his way rejoicing" (Acts 8:39).

Friend, you may never know how God uses you. Philip didn't. He was whisked away by the Holy Spirit, just as quickly as he was brought to this desert road. Philip may have never known the joy that filled this Ethiopian man's life. It says that the Ethiopian never saw Philip again, but "went on his way rejoicing."

Neither did Philip know that the results of this one man's transformation probably touched an entire nation. Early church tradition tells us that this man went back to his homeland and became a powerful evangelist that God used to spark a great spiritual awakening in Ethiopia.

Take Away for Today: Perhaps you work with, go to school with, or live near a person who does not have a relationship with Jesus Christ. With God's guidance and strength, plan your approach to having a spiritual conversation with them about the most important matter in life.

Part VI
Envision ... Living By Faith

ENVISION: You persevere in life's trials by trusting God to sustain you and to bring about His glorious purposes in and through your life. You are strengthened by an ever-increasing love of God and knowledge of His Word. Your trust in God continuously deepens so that you joyfully release yourself and your resources to Him. In faith you obey God's Word, even when you are not sure where it will lead. You are confident that God has a purpose for all the events of your life, whether good or bad. You fight fear and worry with faith in God. You give praise and thanks to God in the difficult circumstances of your life, knowing that He works all things together for His glory and for your good.

SCRIPTURAL FOUNDATION: Matthew 6:19-21; Mark 11:24; Luke 17:6; John 3:16; John 6:29; John 7:38-39; II Corinthians 9:6-12; Philippians 4:4-7; Hebrews 11:6; Hebrews 13:5-6; James 1:2-7; Jude 20.

PART VI ~ DAY 1
FAITH'S FOUNDATION

Today's Scripture Reading: Hebrews 11:1-6

One of primary terms used to describe a Christian in the New Testament is the word "believer." That word underscores the importance of believing, trusting and "faithing" in the life God envisions for us in Christ. Unfortunately this whole concept of faith is very illusive and confusing to us.

There's a powerful illustration of faith in the film, *Indiana Jones and the Last Crusade.* In the film Harrison Ford plays a swashbuckling archeologist named Indiana Jones, who travels around the world searching for treasures. In this case Indiana and his father are on a quest to find the Holy Grail, the cup supposedly used by Christ at the Last Supper and which possesses certain healing powers for those who drink from it. Jones' father is shot and critically injured as the two navigate a maze of obstacles to the location of the Grail. In a riveting scene Jones comes to the edge of a deep chasm. There appears to be no way to cross to the other side. As he studies a book of clues

Indiana Jones realizes, "It's a leap of faith." In the background his father is whispering, "You must believe, boy, you must believe." With those words ringing in his ears Indiana musters his courage, and slowly steps out into the empty air before him. Surprisingly Indiana's foot lands on solid ground. In the movie the camera pulls back to reveal that Indiana is, indeed, standing on a slender stone bridge, which he then sees has been carved in a way so as to match the shape of the chasm below. With a sigh of relief Indiana Jones continues on to the other side where he finds the Holy Grail.

From a biblical perspective faith is a spiritual ability that undergirds everything else in the Christian life. Without faith it is impossible to please God (Hebrews 11:6a). Through faith God uses ordinary people to do extraordinary things. Faith in God enables us to fully give our lives and all that we are to Him. Faith emboldens us to persevere in life's trials as we trust God to sustain us and to bring about His glorious purposes in and through our lives.

Faith, however, is only as valid as the object in which one places their faith. So what is it about God that releases us to put our confidence in Him and surrender our lives and all that we have to Him? We might call this the theological foundation of living by faith.

Our knowledge of God comes through God's revelation of Himself in three ways: Scripture, creation and, most sublimely, Jesus Christ. The Bible is God's inspired *written* revelation of Himself (see II Timothy 3:16). Creation is God's *natural* revelation of Himself (see Romans 1:20). Jesus Christ is God's perfect *personal* revelation of Himself (see Hebrews 1:1-3).

What we learn about God from these sources is the basis for our confidence in Him. Please consider just a few qualities of God which form the foundation of faith.

GOD'S EXISTENCE

For the honest observer God's existence is undeniable. If we seriously consider the grandness of the universe and the intricacies of our own bodies the logical conclusion is that nature didn't just happen; it was caused and created by a Being who had no beginning or end. Of course, that Being is the eternal God. He really exists! But because God is invisible it still requires a measure of faith to accept the fact of His existence. "Anyone who comes to him must believe that he exists..." (Hebrews 11:6b). We will never draw near to someone whom we believe doesn't exist. Yet when we do approach God in faith He rewards us. "And without faith it is impossible to please God, because anyone who comes to him must believe that he exists and that *he rewards those who earnestly seek him*" (Hebrews 11:6, italics mine).

GOD'S POWER

Faith is possible when we are convinced that the object of our faith – the One in whom we are putting our confidence – is powerful enough to do what we cannot do. Again we go back to the natural order which has the fingerprints of God all over it: "For since the creation of the world God's invisible qualities—his eternal power and divine nature—have been clearly seen, being understood from what has been made, so that men are without excuse" (Romans 1:20).

Scripture also reveals God's power. One of the great and powerful acts of God came in history in His deliverance of the nation of Israel. Exodus describes how the Egyptian army was in hot pursuit of the Israelites who had marched out of their life of slavery to the Egyptians. The Israelites, being led along by God Himself, came to the shore of the Red Sea. Where would they go from there? The people panicked, but their faithful and fearless leader Moses raised his staff into the air and the waters of the Red Sea miraculously parted, allowing the entire company of the Israelites to cross over on dry ground. As Pharaoh and his army followed the Israelites into the dry sea bottom, suddenly the invisible walls holding back the waters disappeared and the sea crashed down on the Egyptians, destroying them all.

How was this event to be explained? After their great

deliverance the Israelites had a worship service and Moses composed a new song just for that occasion. His song, found in Exodus 15, exalted the Lord for His tremendous act in behalf of His people, the Israelites. One stanza of Moses' hymn says, "Your right hand, O Lord, was majestic in power. Your right hand, O Lord, shattered the enemy" (Exodus 15:6). Later in the song Moses asks the question: "Who among the gods is like you, O Lord? Who is like you — majestic in holiness, awesome in glory, working wonders?" (Exodus 15:11).

Every day we are confronted with the reality of our weaknesses. We cannot love our mates the way they deserve to be loved. We don't have the wisdom we need to make difficult decisions. We don't have the strength to resist temptation. In those moments we may trust in God who is all-powerful. His Word is replete with promise after promise of His powerful help that is available to those who put their faith in Him.

GOD'S FAITHFULNESS

In the Christian experience our faith is in God, not in our faith. Our faith can only be effective because of the faithfulness of God. We have faith because He is faithful. We trust Him because He is trustworthy. This is sometimes a challenge for us when we have been let down by people who have made promises to us. Trust doesn't come easy for people who have been disappointed by others.

Again we look to God's written revelation of Himself. One quality that He repeatedly reminds us of in His Word is His faithfulness.

"With your mouth you have promised and with your hand you have fulfilled" (II Chronicles 6:15).

"Your kingdom is an everlasting kingdom, and your dominion endures through all generations. The Lord is faithful to all his promises and loving toward all he has made" (Psalm 145:13).

"God, who has called you into fellowship with his Son Jesus Christ our Lord, is faithful" (1 Corinthians 1:9).

Because God is faithful and trustworthy He is not hesitant to require of us complete faith and trust in Himself before we realize the benefits of knowing Him. Faith is the key that unlocks everything else in our relationship with God.

Faith is the very basis for our right-standing with God. On one occasion Jesus was asked about the primary work that was required of humans. "Jesus answered, 'The work of God is this: *to believe* in the one he has sent'" (John 6:29, italics mine). Salvation and eternal life are only ours as we put our faith in Christ. "For it is by grace you have been saved, through faith—and this not from yourselves, it is the gift of God—not by works, so that no one can boast" (Ephesians 2:8).

Take Away for Today: In the words of the father of Indiana Jones as he stood at the brink of the chasm, "You must believe, boy, you must believe." Start today by laying hold of a promise God has made to you in His Word. Cling to that promise in absolute confidence that God will do what He promised.

PART VI ~ DAY 2
ACCESSING THE LIFE

Today's Scripture Reading: Matthew 14:22-33

The life God envisions for us when He brings us into
union with His Son Jesus Christ is accessed by faith. "And
without faith it is impossible to please God, because anyone who comes to him must believe that he exists and
that he rewards those who earnestly seek him" (Hebrews
11:6). The Apostle Paul said, "We live by faith, not by
sight" (2 Corinthians 5:7). The very act of envisioning the
life God plans for us is an act of faith. It is seeing the
unseen. "So we fix our eyes not on what is seen, but on
what is unseen. For what is seen is temporary, but what is
unseen is eternal" (2 Corinthians 4:18).

Likewise, the Bible shows us exactly what faith is: "Now
faith is being sure of what we hope for and certain of what
we do not see" (Hebrews 11:1). What a challenge! Brad
Waggoner explains that, "Faith is not imagination, not
hopeful thinking. Faith is not blind. God has designed the
Christian life in such a manner that we must often act on
His Word without physical manifestations from God." [38]

Here's one definition of faith: Faith is "choosing to live as though God's Word is true, regardless of circumstances, emotions or cultural trends." [39] I would revise this definition slightly. Faith is choosing live *in the assurance* that God's word is true, regardless of circumstances, emotions or cultural trends.

Everything we do in the Christ-life is to be done by faith. We learn and apply the truth of God's Word in the faith that it is indeed the very truth of God and the only right foundation for our life. We obey God and deny self because we believe that what God calls us to do is indeed the right thing. When we serve God and others we do so believing that He is working through us. When we share Jesus Christ with others we trust that the invisible power of the gospel is sufficient to eternally save souls. When we worship we do so in faith believing that God rewards those who diligently seek Him. When we build Christ-centered relationships we do so believing that God has placed those people in our lives for His eternal purposes.

Faith is "choosing to live" a particular way. Faith doesn't come to full fruit until it has moved us to some action, even if that action is simply being still before the Lord (Psalm 46:10). Most of the time faith moves us to choose a particular course of action. To me one of the most astounding acts of faith came in the life of Jesus' main man, the Apostle Peter. It is one of the better known sequences in the life of Jesus. The setting was what was commonly known as the Sea of Galilee (essentially a large lake). Jesus instructed His disciples to get into the boat and go on ahead of Him to the other side of the lake while He went away for a time of solitude and prayer. Meanwhile the disciples, out in the middle of the lake as darkness comes, found themselves engulfed in a fierce storm. Suddenly they saw something that frightened them ... a solitary figure walking towards them on top of the waves. At first they thought it was a ghost. Then Jesus spoke: "Take courage! It is I. Don't be afraid" (Matthew 14:27).

Remember, faith is living in the assurance that God's Word is true, regardless of circumstances or emotions. The words of Jesus are true; now His disciples must decide whether or not they will act in the assurance that His Word is true in the face of challenging circumstances and anxious emotions.

Peter, the leader of the disciples, was the first to respond: "Lord, if it's you ... tell me to come to you on the water" (v.28). Jesus replied to Peter's request with just one word ... "come" (v.29). With that, Peter was over the side of boat and into the water. What was he thinking? He had never done anything like this before. Don't forget that Peter was a fisherman by trade. He knew the laws of the lake. Exactly 100% of those who had attempted to walk on water failed, if anyone was even foolish enough to try. But this time things were different. Jesus had spoken; His

Word was true. Peter could walk on the water to Jesus. Peter acted in the assurance that what Jesus said was true. Taking a huge step of faith Peter found that the waters that normally swallowed up people now were firm beneath his feet. Moving toward Jesus, Peter took one step, then another and another. What a rush of exhilaration he must have felt! I imagine it was like a baby taking his or her first steps toward the outstretched arms of a parent. And for an unspecified period of time Peter lived an entirely supernatural life, walking on water. For however long Peter was out there walking on the water he was living his life totally sustained by the promise and the power of Jesus.

Suddenly something changed. The storm was still just as fierce. The Savior was just as strong. What changed was Peter's thinking ... and his faith. Matthew's account in the gospel reveals that when Peter "saw the wind" he was overwhelmed with fear and began to sink (v.30). The word "saw" doesn't mean that Peter simply saw with his eyes. The word means to see something and to think about or consider it. Peter saw the circumstances and began to consider what was happening from a human perspective. The circumstances hadn't changed; Peter's feelings about them had changed. Peter's faith faltered and immediately he began to sink.

Now how do we know that this was a faith issue for Peter? We know it because Jesus identified it as such. When

Peter cried out to Jesus to rescue him (v.30), Jesus reached out his hand, caught Peter, and then spoke to him: "You of little faith ... why did you doubt?" (v.31). You see, for however long Peter walked on the water he was living by faith. When Peter looked away from Jesus and began to look on the circumstances, doubt overwhelmed him.

Again we don't know how many steps Peter took walking on the water. Yet for those amazing moments Peter lived a totally supernatural life sustained by faith in the promise and the power of God. It was a taste of the life that would be available to him when he was filled with the resurrection power of Jesus Christ through His Holy Spirit. This is the life God had in mind for us when He sent His Son to die on the cross and to be resurrected on the third day.

Take Away for Today: Stop and ponder Peter's experience ... living life totally sustained by the promise and the power of God. That's the life of faith. Look to Jesus in every temptation and trial. As you keep our eyes on Him, riveted to His promises, you will be sustained by His power. The minute that you look away from Jesus ... the minute you begin to think about your circumstances purely from a human perspective ... you are sunk!

PART VI ~ DAY 3
THE PRAYER OF FAITH

Today's Scripture Reading: Luke 18:1-8

Faith is manifested in our prayer and the claiming of the promises of God. Consider a few of the overwhelming admonitions and promises about prayer in God's Word:

"But you, dear friends, build yourselves up in your most holy faith and pray in the Holy Spirit" (Jude 20).

"And the prayer offered in faith will make the sick person well; the Lord will raise him up" (James 5:15a).

"Therefore I tell you, whatever you ask for in prayer, believe that you have received it, and it will be yours" (Mark 11:24)

"But when he asks, he must believe and not doubt, because he who doubts is like a wave of the sea, blown and tossed by the wind" (James 1:6)

If faith is a requirement to answered prayer, how is faith demonstrated in our praying? At the risk of overly simplifying something that is very rich, it essentially boils down to two great activities (persistence and praise) and one great result (peace).

PERSISTENCE

We live in a day of instant results. If results are not immediate we move on to the next solution. The same can hold true in our praying. If we don't see instant answers for what we have asked of the Lord, we give up. Faith is essential to answered prayer, and persistent prayer is evidence of faith.

On one occasion Jesus "told his disciples a parable to show them that they should always pray and not give up" (Luke 18:1). "Always pray and not give up…" Sounds like something I need to learn. The parable involved a widow who needed a judge to step in to justly resolve a dispute with her adversary. The judge was not a very likeable guy, according to Jesus. He didn't fear God or care about people. The widow, however, kept pestering him and for some time the judge refused to act. The widow wouldn't give up and finally the judge gives in to her persistence. He said, "Because this widow keeps bothering me, I will see that she gets justice, so that she won't eventually wear me out with her coming " (Luke 18:5). Now Jesus was not saying that God is like that calloused judge. He is saying that God is *not* like that calloused judge. If it took that kind of persistence to wear down this worldly judge, will not God who is the Righteous Judge, more readily respond to the persistent prayers of His children. Jesus added, "Will not God bring about justice for his chosen ones, who cry out to him day and night? Will he keep putting them off?" (Luke 18:7). The point of Jesus' parable is clear: God responds to persistent prayer.

In another setting Jesus taught His disciples about prayer and He said: "Ask and it will be given to you; seek and you will find; knock and the door will be opened to you. For everyone who asks receives; he who seeks finds; and to him who knocks, the door will be opened" (Matthew 7:7-8).

Of interest is that when Jesus said "ask" He meant "keep on asking. When He said "seek" He meant "keep on seeking." When He said "knock" He meant "keep on knocking."

Persistence in prayer is evidence of our faith. It is not that we think God didn't hear us the first time. We continue to ask as an indication that we are still trusting God to act, even when we have to wait for His perfect timing. "As the eyes of slaves look to the hand of their master, as the eyes of a maid look to the hand of her mistress, so our eyes look to the Lord our God, till he shows us his mercy" (Psalm 123:2). By persistent praying we acknowledge our absolute and complete dependence on God.

Andrew Murray's classic tome on prayer, entitled *With Christ in the School of Prayer*, gives this counsel on persistent praying: "There may be things around us that have to be corrected through prayer before the answer can fully happen. The faith that has, according to the command, believed that it has received, can allow God to take His time. It knows it has and must succeed. In quiet, persistent, and determined perseverance it continues in prayer and thanksgiving until the blessing comes. And so we see a combination of what at first sight appears to be so contradictory: the faith that rejoices in God's answer as a present possession combined with the patience that cries day and night until that answer comes."[40]

PRAISE

Praise in our praying is evidence of our confidence in God. It manifests the reality that we want God, not just the stuff He gives us. Praise in our persistent praying is evidence that our eyes are on Him. Until and when God grants our petition He will be enough for us. The prophet Jeremiah exclaimed, "I say to myself, 'The Lord is my portion; therefore I will wait for him'" (Lamentations 3:24).

One of the great prayers recorded in Scripture came as the apostles in the early church were threatened with persecution if they didn't stop preaching. The apostles returned to the gathering of the church and reported about the threats that had been made, then "they raised their voices together in prayer to God" (Acts 4:24). Now as a pastor I have presided over countless prayer meetings. I know how we typically pray about things like this. We usually barge right into the presence of God with "gimme this and gimme that." But examine carefully the praying of the early church and you get an idea of why they possessed such extraordinary power. Notice how their prayer begins ... it's more about God than it is about their need: "You spoke by the Holy Spirit through the mouth of your servant, our father David: 'Why do the nations rage and the peoples plot in vain? The kings of the earth take their stand and the rulers gather together against the Lord and against his Anointed One.' Indeed Herod and Pontius Pilate met together with the Gentiles and the people of Israel in this city to conspire against your holy servant Jesus, whom you anointed. They did what your power and will had decided beforehand should happen" (Acts 4:25-28).

Only after this great outpouring of praise for God's providence and power did they finally get around to petitioning God for what they needed (see vv.29-30).

PEACE

The glorious outcome of the prayer of faith is peace. When we are absolutely confident in the God to whom we pray we may rest in the assurance that He will come through in time. "You will keep in perfect peace him whose mind is steadfast, because he trusts in you" (Isaiah 26:3).

I recently read a sermon by Pastor Mark Dever in which he recounted a situation that occurred in the life of the famous 18th century preacher Jonathan Edwards. Having led his church in Massachusetts through a time of great revival Edwards was suddenly dismissed from the church over a theological disagreement. We can readily imagine the grief and sadness this must have caused in his life.

Some of you reading this will empathize even more deeply having been through a similar experience of losing a job. Or it might be some other kind of loss ... the loss of a spouse to death or divorce, the loss of trusted friend, or the loss of huge chunk of your savings. It's these kinds of losses that have the potential of shaking the foundation of our very lives.

As he went through the suffering of being fired from his church, Jonathan Edwards knew this peace about which I speak. An eye-witness observed Edwards' response when he was informed by the church council of their action. The observer said, "That faithful witness received the shock, unshaken. I never saw the least symptom of displeasure in his countenance the whole week, but he appeared like a man of God, *whose happiness was out of the reach of his enemies.*" I reckon that the "happiness" the observer mentions is actually the peace about which Jesus spoke.

Powerful prayer springs from confident faith in God that He will be sufficient for us no matter how He chooses to answer our prayer.

Take Away for Today: So how about you? What happens when the troubles of this world land their crushing blows? Is the peace of Jesus running so deeply in your life that it is out of reach of the troubles of this world?

PART VI ~ DAY 4
SUFFERING AND FAITH

Today's Scripture Reading: James 1:2-8

God's Word gives us this guidance as we go through the various trials of life: "Consider it pure joy, my brothers, whenever you face trials of many kinds, because you know that the testing of your faith develops perseverance. Perseverance must finish its work so that you may be mature and complete, not lacking anything" (James 1:2-4).

This truth helps us understand why God permits suffering in our lives. Suffering comes in the form of trials we must face. These trials come in various shapes and sizes. When James speaks of "many kinds of trials," he speaks literally of multi-colored trials. They may touch us at the point of our physical health, our emotional well-being, our financial security, our professional responsibilities, or our spiritual battles.

Trials may last for a few days or for several years, but we are assured that God has such a certain plan for us through the trials that we are told to rejoice in them. What is this plan? Ultimately it is that we will be "mature and complete, not lacking anything" (v.4). This means to be spiritually mature and personally complete in *every* detail, lacking nothing in the way of a fully developed life in Christ.

Big question: Is that the overarching desire of our lives? If it isn't, and if we want mainly to be comfortable and stress-free in life, we will *run from* trials rather than *rejoice in* them. We will *whine* through the trials rather than to *worship* through them.

However, if we have come to the place in our lives where we desire, more than anything else, a life absolutely full of God, we can think on our trials with joy. We understand the connection between our suffering and the glorious purposes of God for our lives.

A key piece in this puzzle is something called perseverance or patient endurance. In God's plans for us we must go through suffering so we can develop this endurance. Why? Because the ultimate purpose of God for us (to be mature and complete) cannot be accomplished until endurance has finished its great work in us.

Endurance is developed by prolonged exposure to pain and strain.

Runners learn this in training for long-distance races. They cannot run for hours on end without endurance … endurance that comes from prolonged exposure to pain and strain. Over time runners add time and intensity to their workouts so the body gradually adapts to the increasing demands put upon it. They will not be able to complete a race until patient endurance has finished its work.

Maybe you have thought something like, "Oh I wish this problem would just go away. I'm tired of dealing with it." I certainly have. Yet if the trial goes away before endurance has finished its work ... if the suffering ends before my faith has been adequately tested and strengthened ... then I will miss God's glorious purpose through the trial. I will miss the life full of God.

Again, the big question is, "Do I want to be spiritually mature and personally complete in Christ more than I want to be free of pain and strain?"

Remember, endurance is developed by *prolonged* exposure to pain and strain. There are no short-cuts. So whether the trial lasts for a few days or several years, we know that God knows exactly how long it takes for our faith to be strengthened and for patient endurance to finish its great work in us.

This process is successful when we learn how to rejoice throughout the prolonged exposure to pain and strain. We must develop the ability to be sustained by God when the fears and worries press in on us so heavily that we can hardly breathe. How can we keep from being absolutely paralyzed by anxiety as we go through trials? We learn the skill described in Philippians 4:6-7: "Do not be anxious about anything, but in everything, by prayer and petition, with thanksgiving, present your requests to God. And the peace of God, which transcends all understanding, will guard your hearts and your minds in Christ Jesus."

Recently a young lady came to my office to explain to my assistant and me that she had received some bad news. She and her fiancé had been making plans to get married the next year. I was honored to have been asked to officiate at their wedding. However, her fiancé began to have second-thoughts about the marriage, and then broke off the engagement. The young lady came by to inform me that I could remove the wedding from my calendar.

As she told us the news it was apparent that her heart was broken. Tears flowed down her cheeks as she told of her continued love for the young man with whom she thought she would be spending the rest of her life. Yet what came through the tears was more than sadness … there was amazing faith. She talked of how God was teaching her about His ministry to the broken-hearted. She quoted Psalm 51:8: "Let me hear joy and gladness; let the bones you have crushed rejoice." She marveled that bones that were crushed by sorrow could dance with joy and gladness once again.

Earlier that day I heard a song on Christian radio that gripped my attention. I remembered only a few lines from the song, and tried to repeat them (not sing them!) to her. Imagine my amazement when the broken-hearted young lady began to recite the words of nearly the whole song from memory. She had clung to those very same Scripture-based words over the last several days as she went through the pain of deep disappointment. The song, entitled "Blessings," by Sarah Story, carries an incredible message:

> We pray for blessings, we pray for peace
> Comfort for family, protection while we sleep
> We pray for healing, for prosperity
> We pray for Your mighty hand to ease our suffer-
> ing
>
> All the while, You hear each spoken need
> Yet love us way too much to give us lesser things
>
> Cause what if Your blessings come through rain-
> drops?
> What if Your healing comes through tears
> What if a thousand sleepless nights
> Are what it takes to know You're near?
>
> What if trials of this life
> Are Your mercies in disguise?
>
> We pray for wisdom, Your voice to hear
> We cry in anger when we cannot feel You near
> We doubt Your goodness, we doubt Your love
> As if every promise from Your Word is not enough
>
> And all the while You hear each desperate plea

And long that we'd have faith to believe

Cause what if Your blessings come through rain-
drops
What if Your healing comes through tears?
What if a thousand sleepless nights
Are what it takes to know You're near?

And what if trials of this life
Are Your mercies in disguise

When friends betray us, when darkness seems to
win
We know the pain reminds this heart
That this is not, this is not our home
It's not our home

Cause what if Your blessings come through rain-
drops
What if Your healing comes through tears?
And what if a thousand sleepless nights
Are what it takes to know You're near?

What if my greatest disappointments
Or the aching of this life
Is the revealing of a greater thirst
This world can't satisfy?

And what if trials of this life
The rain, the storms, the hardest nights
Are Your mercies in disguise?

There's something very cavernous in those words, "What if my greatest disappointments, or the aching of this life, is the revealing of a greater thirst this world can't satisfy." This may be hard for any of us to believe, but it's worth whatever pain God has to bring us through in order to teach us that awesome, liberating truth.

When Jesus went through fiery trials He "entrusted himself to him who judges justly" (I Peter 2:23b). So we can also entrust ourselves into God's righteous hands as we have to endure various trials. James 1:2 says to "consider it pure joy, my brothers, when you face trials of many kinds..." As hard as it may seem, we can actually jump up and down for joy when we go through adversity because we know that it is a signal that God is up to something great.

Take Away for Today: So "in case of fire" keep putting your life into the hands of God. Rejoice in your sufferings because you know that God is working something through those trials that will be glorious in the end.

PART VI ~ DAY 5
TRUST AND OBEY

Today's Scripture Reading: Exodus 16:1-12

A vivid memory from my childhood comes from an experience where I learned one of my first lessons in faith. My buddies and I were playing baseball in the front yard of my house when someone hit the ball up on the roof of our garage. Because the roof was flat the ball didn't roll back to the ground, so someone had to go up after it. Since it was my house it became my duty to go up on the roof. We had no ladder so one of my taller friends boosted me up on his shoulders and I scrambled up the nine or ten feet on to the garage roof, retrieved the ball, went back to the edge expecting to be helped down by my "friends." There was no one in sight. They thought it would be funny to leave me on the roof with no way to get down. I began to yell for help, but to no avail. Soon my dad heard all the noise and came outside to see what was up. When he saw my predicament he chuckled, then just held up his arms and said, "Jump." Immediately I was confronted with a dilemma. Do I trust my dad and jump into his arms, or do

I stay on the roof for the rest of my life? It really was not a big decision. I obeyed … and jumped! Why? Because I had absolute confidence in my dad. I knew that he loved me and *wanted* to catch me when I jumped into his arms. Furthermore I knew that he was strong and that he *could* catch me when I jumped into his arms.

That was a traumatic experience for a little guy, and I guess that's why I've never forgotten it. It has served as a repeated reminder to me of what it means to trust and obey.

Has it occurred to you that every command in the Bible is also an invitation to trust God?

After God powerfully delivered the Israelites through the Red Sea they embarked upon four decades of travelling in the Sinai wilderness. Biblical scholars estimate that the community of Israel numbered in the millions, counting men, women and children. Being in the wilderness, where would that many people find enough food to eat? By the abundant, miraculous provision of God. The people, however, were required to trust and obey.

First came the provision of God: "Then the Lord said to Moses, 'I will rain down bread from heaven for you…'" (Exodus 16:4a). God's plan was to drop what later is called "manna" from the heavens. When the thin flakes first appeared on the ground the Israelites had never seen anything like it. They asked, "What is it?" (v.15), which in Hebrew sounds like "manna."

Then came the instructions from God. "The people

are to go out each day and gather enough for that day. In this way I will test them and see whether they will follow my instructions" (Exodus 16:4b). In obeying God's instruction in this they would demonstrate that they trusted God that He would provide for them in the same way the next day. They did not need to hoard it. Those who doubted God soon found that He meant what He said. If someone picked up more than they needed for a regular day, when they tried to eat it the next day they found that it had rotted.

God did, however, make an exception for the Sabbath, a day they were not to do any kind of work. Again they were to trust and obey. If they trusted God enough to obey Him by not working on the Sabbath, He would provide. On the day before the Sabbath the Lord provided enough for two days so they would not have to go out and gather food (work) on the Sabbath.

The reason God did this was to build the faith of His people, something far more important to Him than anything else in their lives. Their faith would be evidenced by their obedience to God.

When we obey a command of God we are demonstrating trust in at least three ways.

First, when we obey we trust that God's ways are always right. Of the many examples I could use from Scripture, I will just focus on two with which many believers struggle in trusting God: sexual purity and financial generosity.

God commands that we should avoid sexual immorality (I Thessalonians 4:3). When we obey that command we are trusting that God is right in demanding that of us. On the other hand, the world says that it is perfectly acceptable to do the opposite ... to engage in sexual immorality. Which view do I believe is right? When I obey the command of the Lord I am trusting that His Word is true and His ways are right.

Or consider the matter of financial stewardship. God, in His Word, repeatedly commands us to be sacrificial and generous in giving financially to His Kingdom's work. In the Old Testament this was typically spoken of in terms of giving a tenth (tithe) of one's income to God's work. "Bring the whole tithe into the storehouse, that there may be food in my house. Test me in this," says the Lord Almighty..." (Malachi 3:10). In the New Testament the Lord moves beyond a rigid percentage to an unlimited surrender of all our resources into the hands of God in faith. Still our giving is to be in proportion the blessings of God in our lives. "On the first day of every week, each one of you should set aside a sum of money in keeping with his income, saving it up, so that when I come no collections will have to be made" (1 Corinthians 16:2).

When we obey these commands of Scripture related to the use of our finances we do so trusting that God is right in demanding this of us. To disobey in this matter reveals our doubts about the rightness of God.

Second, when we obey we trust that God loves us. Again, using the example of sexual immorality, it would be easy for us to think that God simply wants to make life miserable for us when he tells us not to engage in sex outside of marriage. But when we obey His command we are saying to Him that we trust that He has our best interest in mind when He prohibited that behavior.

Again, think about the matter of financial stewardship in this regard. When we give generously, sacrificially and proportionally to the Lord and His work we do so out of obedience. That obedience is rooted in the faith that God, by putting these limits on our lives, reveals His love for us. Faithful giving breaks the grip of greed and covetousness in our lives. "Keep your life free from love of money, and be content with what you have, for he has said, 'I will never leave you nor forsake you.' So we can confidently say, 'The Lord is my helper; I will not fear; what can man do to me?'" (Hebrews 13:5-6). The Lord never leaves us or fails to help us because He loves us.

Third, when we obey we trust that God will reward us for obedience. Sometimes the reward is immediate. In Deuteronomy Moses restates the Lord's commands for His people as they prepare to enter the Promised Land. These commands included how they were to behave in sexual purity. At the conclusion of this the Lord through Moses promises this: "All these blessings will come upon you and accompany you if you obey the Lord your God"

(Deuteronomy 28:2). When we obey the Lord we are trusting in the goodness of God to reward and bless those have faith to obey.

In the matter of financial stewardship the Lord promises to provide for our needs as we give to His work. After commanding the Israelites to give the tithe, the Lord promised: "'Test me in this,' says the Lord Almighty, 'and see if I will not throw open the floodgates of heaven and pour out so much blessing that you will not have room enough for it'" (Malachi 3:10b). In terms of New Testament giving the Lord promises: "Remember this: Whoever sows sparingly will also reap sparingly, and whoever sows generously will also reap generously" (2 Corinthians 9:6).

Granted, God's rewards for obedience may not come immediately, but sooner or later we will reap the benefits of doing things God's way. At the very least we know that one day all right will be rewarded. Until that day we continue to trust and obey.

Take Away for Today: When the Israelites trusted God to provide, and followed His instructions they were blessed to awaken every day to find the manna awaiting them. For forty years God taught them to obey, living day by day by faith. Try that today. Live hour by hour this day in faith.

PART VII
ENVISION ... HONORING GOD IN WORSHIP

ENVISION: You acknowledge God alone as worthy of all worship. You genuinely revere Him for His glory and His holiness. You maintain a conversational relationship with God through various forms of private prayer and worship each day. You gather regularly and wholeheartedly with God's people to worship Him publicly. As an act of worship you fully offer yourself and all that you have to God. Your heart is full of passion for the glory of God. You are drawn to the invitation of God to seek, know and love Him. You regularly experience God in worship. In public worship you strive to keep your thoughts focused on God. You recognize that in public worship God alone is the audience. You approach God through the righteousness of Christ and glory in the excellence of Christ. The reason you live your life is to honor and glorify God.

SCRIPTURAL FOUNDATION: Deut.4:29; 6:4-5; Matt.6:5-18; John 4:23-24; Acts 2:46-47; Rom.12:1; I Cor.10:31; Eph.5:18-21; Col.3:16-17; I Thess.5:16-18; I Tim.2:1-10; Heb.13:15-16

PART VII ~ DAY 1
THE TRUE SEEKER IN WORSHIP

Today's Scripture Reading: John 4:1-14

In recent years many church leaders have focused on a group of people known as "seekers." Seekers, as the name implies, are people who may be far from God but seem to have a longing to know God. So churches began to explore ways to make their church experience, including worship services and need-based programs, more "seeker friendly." The idea is to help non-believers feel more comfortable in a church setting, and to show how the gospel is relevant to their lives. No doubt, many have come through the doors of churches and into a relationship with Jesus Christ because of these efforts.

It is not wrong to keep human seekers in mind as we conduct our life as the church. It is wrong, however, to make the human seeker the starting point in our approach to church, including worship experiences. The fact is that authentic worship only happens when we understand that there is one True Seeker in worship, and that is the Lord God who created all things with the goal of gaining glory for Himself. He has placed within each human soul a hunger to know and experience the living God. This communion happens in spiritual worship.

Jesus' encounter with the Samaritan woman in John 4 underscores this. Recall that Jesus came to a well in the region of Samaria where He met a woman who had come there to draw water. It was a divine appointment. This woman was confused about worship because Samaritans possessed a view of worship that differed from the biblical worship God gave to the Jews. Jesus said to the woman: "A time is coming and has now come when the true worshipers will worship the Father in spirit and truth, for they are the kind of worshipers *the Father seeks.* God is spirit, and his worshipers must worship in spirit and in truth" (John 4:23-24, italics mine).

God, through Jesus Christ, was about to bring worship to the level that it had never reached before. Through the work of Christ in His crucifixion and resurrection, and by the gift of the Holy Spirit, God would make worship something that was not just external. The human heart would become a temple of the Holy Spirit in which true praise and worship would be offered through the Spirit. Christ-followers are those who "worship by the Spirit of God, who glory in Christ Jesus, and who put no confidence in the flesh…" (Philippians 3:3).

When human beings seek glory for themselves it is not an admirable attribute. But it is different with God. For

God to seek glory for Himself testifies to the fact that He is true. God knows that no other in all creation is worthy of worship. God is complete in His holiness. His glory is the outshining of all His excellencies. He alone is worthy of worship.

So worship doesn't begin with us. If we don't understand this we will always miss the mark of the authentic kind of worship prescribed for us in the Scriptures. Biblical worship doesn't begin with us seeking God ... it begins with God seeking us. He displays His magnificence in all creation with the intent that all creation would be drawn to give Him glory.

God is a self-revealing God. The only way we know anything about the worthiness of God to receive worship is because He has chosen to reveal Himself to us. God's creation of the universe invites us to seek Him in worship (see Romans 1:18-20). In Scripture God revealed His multi-faceted attributes and activity which are designed to cause us to worship (see Revelation 15:4). Also God's engagement in history is designed to elicit worshipful seeking by all whom He has graciously blessed (see Acts 17:24-28).

God created us with the intellectual capacity to observe certain things and to draw conclusions. As we honestly observe creation and cultures the logical conclusion is that God exists and has graciously ordered the world for His glory and for the good of His creatures. There is, however, something broken in us that keeps us from moving from this conclusion to actual worship. It is called sin, and it's the reason God sent His Son to be the Savior of the world.

Louie Giglio, in his book *The Air I Breathe*, says, "We are all worshipers, created to bring pleasure and honor to the God who made us. You may not consider yourself a 'worshiping' kind of person, but you cannot help but worship ... something. It's what you were made to do. Should you for some reason choose not to give God what He desires, you'll worship anyway – simply exchanging the Creator for something He has created. " [41]

God's most sublime revelation of Himself has come in the person of His Son, Jesus Christ. "In the past God spoke to our forefathers through the prophets at many times and in various ways, but in these last days he has spoken to us by his Son, whom he appointed heir of all things, and through whom he made the universe" (Hebrews 1:1-2). God sent His Son into the world to reveal His glory. "The Word became flesh and made his dwelling among us. We have seen his glory, the glory of the One and Only, who came from the Father, full of grace and truth" (John 1:14). God's glory causes Him to be glorified by all creation.

For New Testament believers worship now happens in and through the Lord Jesus Christ. The life God envisions for us is found completely in His Son, Jesus Christ. The Father so treasures His Son that the Father is honored when the Son is worshipped. God exalted Jesus to the highest position and gave to Him "the name that is above every name, that at the name of Jesus every knee should bow, and every tongue confess that Jesus Christ is Lord, to the glory of God the Father" (Philippians 2:9-11).

David Bryant and Richard Ross sum up God's desire and design in this way: "Beginning 2000 years ago He has chosen to reveal Himself most clearly in His Son. This is a perfect plan since the Son is the radiance of God's glory and the exact representation of His nature. When the Son had made purification of sins, He was enthroned at the right hand of the Majesty on high. The Father then announced that in this age of the church God the Son is to have supremacy." [42]

So as Christ-followers we have no higher purpose than to treasure (worship) Jesus Christ. I am so eager for your life to be infused with this vision of who Christ is in all of His glory and excellence … and not just in your Sunday worship, but in your lifestyle throughout the week.

One well-known worship leader makes these observations about the state of worship in the hearts and minds of many believers as it relates to the supremacy of Christ: "Often it feels to me as if, for many of our people, singing praise songs and hymns on a Sunday morning has turned into an affair with Christ … Too many of us are far more passionate about lesser, temporal concerns such as getting ahead at the office, finding personal happiness in a hobby, driving a new car, or rearing well-balanced children. But we rarely ever get that excited about Christ Himself, at least on any consistent basis, except when we enter a sanctuary on a Sunday. Then for a while we end up sort of 'swooning' over Christ with feel-good music and heart-stirring prayers – only to return to the daily grind of secular seductions to which, for all practical, purposes, we're thoroughly 'married' ... Christ is more like a 'mistress' to us. He is someone with whom we have the periodic affairs to reinvigorate our spirit so we can return, refreshed, to engage all the other agendas that dominate us most of the time." [43]

Heaven's throne room vision enthralled John in the Revelation: "And they sang a new song: 'You are worthy to take the scroll and to open its seals, because you were slain, and with your blood you purchased men for God from every tribe and language and people and nation.' ... In a loud voice they sang: 'Worthy is the Lamb, who was slain, to receive power and wealth and wisdom and strength and honor and glory and praise!' Then I heard every creature in heaven and on earth and under the earth and on the sea, and all that is in them, singing: 'To him who sits on the throne and to the Lamb be praise and honor and glory and power, for ever and ever!'" (Revelation 5:9, 12-13).

This is the destiny toward which all of history is moving. Christ's glorious reign, however, is not something in the far-off future; it is every bit as real now as it will be then.

Take Away for the Day: Keep this in mind throughout this week. What if you experienced worship on Sunday in such a way that you left the place of worship fired up and eager to walk into the next six days looking for increased displays of Christ's dominion around them? What if you returned to church the next Sunday alive with the realization of Christ's supremacy? What would your worship look like?

PART VII ~ DAY 2
SO WHAT IS WORSHIP?

Today's Scripture Reading: John 4:15-26

When asked about the greatest and most important commandment of God, Jesus replied: "Love the Lord your God with all your heart and with all your soul and with all your mind" (Matthew 22:37). This "Great Commandment" is the foundation of a life of worship for all Christ-followers.

Worship is our response to what we value most. Webster's dictionary: "Worship is extreme devotion or intense love or admiration of any kind." In this sense, we are all worshippers, whether we are Christ-followers or not. Everyone worships what they value most.

As I wrote in the preceding chapter, worship doesn't start with us. It's a response to something that started with God. He reveals Himself; we respond. He discloses; we respond. He unveils; we respond. He shows us amazing things and we respond, "God, You're amazing."

Louie Giglio defines worship in this way: "Worship is our response, both personal and corporate, to God for who He is and what He has done, expressed in and by the things we say and the way we live." [44] In my opinion that definition hits really close to what we read in the Bible about authentic worship.

Focus for a moment on some of the phrases in that definition.

"Worship is our response ... to God"

Worship is a verb as well as a noun. It is something we do. It is not a spectator activity, but one in which the whole person is engaged in responding to God's revelation of Himself. Worship isn't something we watch as when we attend church. Unfortunately, the architecture in many churches communicates this. Worship isn't something we attend like a movie or a concert. Worship is participatory.

"Both personal and corporate"

Worship starts out as something personal and private. If it doesn't start there then corporate worship is hypocritical. However, if our personal worship is not regularly blended with the worship of other believers, our worship is incomplete. So the goal each week for those of us who are serious about honoring God in our worship is for us to bring our worship with us to church.

"To God for who He is"

This is about a relationship. Worship is one person responding to another Person. When we understand by the Scriptures or by creation something about God we are to offer praise to Him. The Bible repeatedly calls upon us to "praise His name." To praise the name of the Lord is to praise His person and His attributes.

When my children were little I made it a practice when I travelled to bring home a gift for them. Without fail, when I walked through the door they would run to meet me, and before long out would come the words, "Daddy, what did you bring me?" They were kids, and I understood. I was happy to see their joy in that moment, but I contrast their greeting with the one I received from my wife, Nan. She would simply say something like, "Welcome home. I'm really glad to see you." My children were glad to see my gifts; my wife was glad to see me.

Imagine how God must feel when He discerns that our desire is more for the things He gives us rather than for who He is.

"To God for … what He has done"

God reveals Himself through His powerful deeds. We, the witnesses and recipients of those deeds, are to respond with thanksgiving. As the psalmist says, "Enter his gates with thanksgiving and his courts with praise; give thanks to him and praise his name" (Psalm 100:4). Our thanksgiving to God must be continuous; every breath we take is a gift from Him.

"Expressed in and by the things we say"

Worship that lingers in our heads and hearts but never making to our lips is counterfeit worship. A casual reading of the hymnbook of the Bible, the Psalms, reveals repeated exhortations to express our worship verbally. Unexpressed gratitude is ingratitude. Unexpressed praise is indifference. We have not reached authentic worship until our praise and thanksgiving move from our heart to our lips. The psalmist said, "My tongue will speak of your righteousness and of your praises all day long" (Psalm 35:28)

"Expressed in and by ... the way we live"

Our worship flows from our hearts to our lips ... and then to our lives. Every act of life is to be offered to the Lord as worship to Him. This means that worship is not just something that happens on Sundays; it's a 24/7 experience. The Apostle Paul exhorts us: "I urge you, brothers, in view of God's mercy, to offer your bodies as living sacrifices, holy and pleasing to God—this is your spiritual act of worship" (Romans 12:1). Our home life, our work life, our recreational life, our financial life, indeed, our entire life is to be an offering of worship to our great God and King.

One Sunday in our church I preached a message on worship. To introduce my message I played a little trick on our congregation. In those days NFL Hall of Fame quarterback Troy Aikman played for the Dallas Cowboys. I told the people that during the preceding week I had played golf at well-known golf club (true). After the round I walked back to my car to put my clubs in the trunk (true). I noticed a man getting out of a luxury SUV parked next to me. Imagine my surprise when it turned out to be Troy Aikman (*not* true). I spun the story more dramatically by telling the audience that I struck up a conversation with Mr. Aikman (*not* true) and introduced myself to him as the pastor of the Travis Avenue Baptist Church. When he heard the name of our church he told me that he knew of our church (probably *not* true). In fact, Troy said that he would like to visit our church some Sunday, to which I replied with an invitation, "How about this Sunday?" He said, "Great. See you Sunday" (*not* true).

At this point most of my church members were hooked. Then I dropped a big one on them by saying, "And, church, I'm happy to say that Mr. Troy Aikman is with us today in our worship service. Troy, please stand and let us welcome you." There was a collective, audible gasp of excitement. Folks were on the edge of their seats; some even stood in order to catch a glimpse of the celebrity. People began to excitedly crane their necks back and forth to see where the famous athlete was standing. I think a few worshippers nearly fell out of the balcony looking for Troy! After a short pause for dramatic effect I sprang the truth on them. Troy Aikman was *not* present; I was "pulling their leg," as we say in Texas.

I took the opportunity to have a little fun with them: "You should have seen some of your faces when you actually thought that Troy Aikman was in the house." I went on to gently remind them that every time we gather as a church to worship, someone far more famous, far more important, than Troy Aikman is present. Almighty God is present when we assemble as the church in His Name. Do we gather with the same sense of awe, excitement and expectancy? Are we on the edge of our seats eager to encounter God in all of His glory? Do our hearts beat a little faster knowing that Someone with that much renown is actually present with us?

We laughed about that episode for several weeks. Yet I hope we all remember the truth for much longer than that. Worship is a true privilege for us to bring our offerings of praise to the great King of the Universe.

Take Away for Today: Remember that when you gather with God's people on the next Lord's Day for worship you are coming into the presence of a holy God. Let that shake you to your very core. Every time you walk into a worship service you are having an encounter with a holy God. Let that fill you with awe and wonder.

PART VII ~ DAY 3
OUR PRIVATE WORSHIP

Today's Scripture Reading: I Thessalonians 5:16-18

When we consider worship we most always think of the public expression of worship when we attend church on Sundays. That corporate experience of worship takes on greater power when we bring our worship with us to church. Stop to think about how different our worship services would be if we all gathered having worshipped privately the other six days of the week.

All of the great men and women of the Bible encountered God on a personal and private level. Read the account in Isaiah 6 of the mighty prophet's exposure to the awesome glory of God. The life of worship that God envisions for followers of His Son includes worshipping "in spirit and in truth" (John 4:23-24). In other words it is something intensely personal. Yes, much of our worshipping life occurs in tandem with other believers; but that must not preclude our private worship.

Jesus, being the very Son of God, experienced private worship of His Father in heaven. I encourage you to read the lengthiest recorded prayer of Jesus in John 17. Notice the many ways in which Jesus expressed His own personal worship of the Father in His private praying. When we worship in the sanctuary of our own souls we are following in the steps of our Savior.

Here are some essentials to building personal worship into the routine of your life each day:

First, read God's Word with an eye for His glory. Often our Bible reading and study is rather self-absorbed. Yet every time you open your Bible you are having an encounter with God, whether you realize it or not. Often we read God's Word with an eye for things that benefit us … guidance for a decision, comfort in our sorrow, or encouragement in our weaknesses. And there's certainly nothing wrong with reading Scripture in that way. Remember that God's Word is the written revelation of Himself, as well as His plans for eternity. Our daily exposure to the Word of God will show us things that are true about God. As we read those truths we should be quick to worship. The psalmist exclaimed, "Seven times a day I praise you for your righteous laws" (Psalm 119:164). Those "righteous laws" reveal the very character of our righteous God.

Second, meditate upon and memorize Scriptures that extol God. Earlier in this book we learned the tremendous value of Scripture memory and meditation. When we memorize verses that specifically reveal the character of God we can readily recite those verse right back to God in worship. Again, the psalmist stated, "I meditate on your precepts and consider your ways" (Psalm 119:15). I love reciting Psalm 13:5-6 in my personal worship: "But I trust in your unfailing love; my heart rejoices in your salvation. I will sing to the Lord, for he has been good to me." If we are to worship in spirit and in truth, there is nothing more true than the Word of God.

Third, front-load your praying with praise, adoration and thanksgiving. It is so easy for us to barge into the presence of God with our demands in prayer. A prerequisite to answered prayer is faith; and praise is the voice of our faith. I think about godly King Hezekiah who faced the ominous threats of the Sennacherib, the king of Assyria. When Hezekiah was handed the threatening letter from Sennacherib he took it immediately into the Temple and spread it out before the Lord. I suspect that my prayer would have started with something like, "O God, I'm in a mess. Help me!" Hezekiah's prayer started differently: "Hezekiah prayed to the Lord: 'O Lord, God of Israel, enthroned between the cherubim, you alone are God over all the kingdoms of the earth. You have made heaven and earth'" (2 Kings 19:15). Do you see the difference?

Fourth, speak the praises of God in conversations with others. While this is not necessarily private worship, it is personal. In chats throughout the day we have the opportunity to exalted God. King David promised, "My tongue will speak of your righteousness and of your praises all day long" (Psalm 35:28). What is on my mind will ultimately come out in my conversations. I am sad to say that even as a pastor I have many conversations throughout the day where I could have given glory to God, but I didn't. That is a missed opportunity to personally worship.

Fifth, let God-exalting, Christ-honoring and Spirit-filled music prompt your worship. The Bible teaches us to "sing and make music in your heart to the Lord" (Ephesians 5:19). With the great proliferation of Christian music today there are plenty of options for just about any taste in music. Let the music provide wings for you to fly into the presence of the Lord in worship. As a runner I most often have earphones connected to Christian music playing on my iPhone. The miles pass much more quickly when I am "lost in wonder, love and praise."

The Bible says, "Do you not know that your body is a temple of the Holy Spirit, who is in you, whom you have received from God? You are not your own; you were bought at a price. Therefore honor God with your body" (1 Corinthians 6:19-20). As a Christ-follower you are indwelt by the Spirit of Christ; your very life is a sanctuary where the God dwells. What happens in a temple or sanctuary? Worship.

Perhaps this is very difficult for you these days because you are suffering in some way. Because of your troubles you're finding it nearly impossible to give praise and thanks to God. I'm reminded of an episode in the life of

Corrie ten Boom, a Dutch believer whose family hid Jews during the Nazi German occupation of Holland. Her family's secret mission was soon discovered by the Germans. Corrie and her sister Betsie were eventually sent to the infamous Ravensbruck concentration camp. The conditions were atrocious with 1400 women crammed into barracks built for 400. Their beds were made of dirty, flea-infested straw. Sores from flea bites covered the bodies of the women.

In her book, *The Hiding Place*, Corrie ten Boom explained that the only bright spot in their tortuous days came at night when they would collapse in their bunks and quietly read from the Bible they had managed to smuggle into the barracks. If the guards discovered the Bible the prisoners would be certainly brutalized, if not killed. So as they studied their Bible the prisoners posted a lookout at the door to alert them if any guards approached.

On one occasion Betsie read from I Thessalonians 5:18: "Give thanks in all circumstances." Betsie challenged the other women to put this verse into practice by naming the things for which they were thankful. The women began to count their blessings. When it came around to Betsie she surprised the other women by giving thanks for the suffocating room ... and the fleas! Corrie rebelled at this: "There's no way even God can make me grateful for a flea." Betsie's faithful spirit, however, prevailed. Corrie said, "And so we stood between piers of bunks and gave thanks for fleas. But this time I was sure Betsie was wrong." [45]

The women enjoyed their daily time of studying the Bible. Strangely, no guards ever entered the barracks to inspect what the women were doing. Soon they were able to have two times of Bible study each day. It wasn't until several months later that they learned that the reason the guards never entered their barracks was because of the infestation of fleas. Yes, worship can happen in a stifling room filled with fleas when you understand that God is gracious, merciful and loving. He's at work, even in the worst of circumstances.

Take Away for Today: If you've typically thought of worship as something you do only on Sundays, try interjecting worship in the various parts of your day. Look for ways to turn your heart and mind to the Lord throughout the traffic pattern of your daily routine.

PART VII ~ DAY 4
OUR PUBLIC WORSHIP

Today's Scripture Reading: Acts 2:42-47

I write this chapter having just attended a Sunday worship service at the church my wife and I often attend when we are on vacation in the mountains. As a pastor I always strive to be a worshipper even when I am leading worship in our church. On a few occasions each year I get to worship without the weight of the responsibility of worship leadership on my mind. I love pastoral ministry, but I also cherish those occasional opportunities to worship from the pew rather than the platform. It gives me an opportunity to practice what I preach and teach.

The New Testament ascribes great importance to corporate worship for the Christ-follower. "Let us not give up meeting together, as some are in the habit of doing, but let us encourage one another—and all the more as you see the Day approaching" (Hebrews 10:25).

Rick Warren puts it this way: "In corporate worship, we worship in ways we are unable to by ourselves. As we sing and celebrate together, pray and confess together, share and meditate together, give offerings and commit together, our faith is reaffirmed, our hope is reinforced, and our life is renewed. That can only happen in community." [46]

While we don't have an existing "order of service" from a worship service of the church in New Testament times, we can discern certain commonalities in their corporate gatherings. We know that corporate worship for the early church was rooted in the Jewish synagogue, since many of the first disciples were Jewish. But the book of Acts and the Epistles show us that the church soon placed their primary emphasis on the Lord's Day (Sunday) and on gathering at various times throughout the week. The early church seldom had the benefit of a dedicated building, so they met primarily in homes. Worship was a part of their gatherings.

The New Testament gives us the following key components to corporate worship: Scripture reading (Acts 2:42; I Timothy 4:13); preaching/teaching of Scripture (I Timothy 5:17; 2 Timothy 4:2); observance of the ordinances of baptism (Matthew 28:19-20) and the Lord's Supper (Acts 2:42; I Corinthians 11:23-26); prayer (Matthew 21:13; Acts 2:42); various expressions of music and singing (Ephesians 5:19; Colossians 3:16); offerings (I Corinthians 16:1-2); and a call to commitment by believers and non-believers (1 Corinthians 14:24-25). All these components must be maintained with Christ-centeredness (Hebrews 10:19-22). Everything is to be done in a "fitting and orderly way" (1 Corinthians 16:40).

For our purposes in this chapter I intend to focus not so much on what happens on the platform or stage in public worship, but what happens in seats where the congregation sits. Worship leaders are responsible for assisting God's people to engage in authentic corporate worship. To do that requires prayerful and deliberate preparation and planning. The same thing is true for all worshippers who gather with God's people on the Lord's Day and on other occasions to exalt Almighty God.

On this day as I worshipped with a local church away from my home church I tried to consciously focus on these aspects of corporate worship among the community of believers:

I tried to stay mentally engaged every moment of the experience. It is so easy to let my mind drift to things that do not relate to the worship of God and the edification of others. I resisted the urge to look at my watch, even though I was beginning to feel hungry and ready for lunch. I'm coming to focus on the Lord, not on anything or anyone else. I want to come wholeheartedly into God's presence.

I tried to respond with the spirit of each song. A conscientious worship leader will blend songs that reflect the various moods of the human spirit (quiet, upbeat, etc.). In the case of our worship today we sang a celebration song at the beginning of the service; I deliberately rejoiced in the Lord. Later when we moved into a more contemplative song, I let my heart be moved in that direction.

I tried to stay focused on the lyrics of each song. One of the songs we sang today was new to me. I struggled a bit with the melody at times, but with my mind I could still reflect upon and rejoice in the truth contained in the lyrics.

I tried to silently pray along with those who prayed aloud. If we are not careful in times of corporate prayer, when another person is praying aloud, our minds can easily drift. We must resist that tendency. As another is voicing prayer to the Lord the rest of us should listen carefully to their words and, with our lips or in our spirit, voice "Amen," or "Yes, Lord." This is the meaning of agreement in prayer.

I tried to allow myself to be emotionally moved by the Lord. Worship is not a funeral; it's a festival. In many circles it is acceptable to get excited about anything but God. If I truly mean what I am saying when I sing, how can my heart not be moved at times either to rejoicing or to brokenness?

I tried to remember that I was coming into worship primarily to give, not receive. I have no agenda except to minister to the Lord and His people. If I get a blessing from it, fine. But that's not the point of my coming to worship. Actually there is only one in the audience of worship … God. All that really matters is whether or not He is pleased with what I offer to Him.

I tried not to focus on human errors or personal differences in worship. No worship service goes off without a glitch. Sometimes those glitches can be distracting, but we must persevere with our focus on the Lord. I chose not to think critically of others in the worship service today who expressed their worship in a different way than I'm comfortable with. My focus is not on them but on God.

I tried to listen for the voice of God in the pastor's message. God was speaking to everyone in the worship service this morning, including me. I tried to rejoice in the truth of God's Word. I tried to think, "Lord, what are you saying to me today through your servant?"

I tried to be responsive at the conclusion of the message. Like many pastors the Lord's messenger today called people to various kinds of commitment. This particular message had a strong evangelistic appeal to it. I prayed for any non-believers who were present and who needed to put their trust in Christ. I prayed for the man on the row in front of me who remained seated with his headed in his hands.

In each of these instances I deliberately stated that I "tried" to worship in this way. I fully understand that as human beings it isn't always easy to worship properly. God looks upon our hearts and knows our desire.

A corporate worship experience is an amazing and awesome thing. Just think about it! Jesus promised this to His followers: "For where two or three come together in my name, there am I with them" (Matthew 18:20). To gather in the name of Jesus is to gather with the purpose of focusing upon His Person and His purposes. When that occurs Jesus promises something astounding. He will be in the midst of those worshippers. Isn't that what we all want and need?

In his book entitled *Soul Shaping* Jim Wilson talks about the spiritual disciplines that conform us to the image of Christ, one of those being corporate worship. He frankly and humbly describes the heart-cry of many pastors as they prepare each week to lead their people in worship:

"So today I'm going to stand before you. Not because I'm better than you or smarter than you or wiser than you or more spiritual than you. I'm going to stand before you because I know this could be the week. This could be the week when we do more than have a worship service. It could be the week when we forget about me and we forget about you and we focus on Him and we truly worship.

"But today I'm standing here, where I'd rather not

be. In a few minutes I'll stand before you and wrestle with every distraction to keep your attention on this message. I'm supposed to be thought-provoking yet lighthearted, brilliant yet humble, thorough yet concise, timeless yet up-to-date.

"And so I pray, 'Let the fire fall, Lord! Bless us; drench us in Your grace! Descend on us with power! Let Your Spirit fill this place!'"

"I'm standing here because I don't know where else to stand. It is my destiny, my calling. But then again, this isn't about me; and it isn't about you, for that matter. It's about Him. So today I stand before you – no, make that beside you – before a holy God who is worthy of our worship and longs for us to come to church prepared to worship Him.

"Could today be the day?" [47]

Take Away for Today: Let's come each Lord's Day with the anticipation that today just might be the day God breaks forth in glory and power in our lives and in our church.

PART VII ~ DAY 5
WORSHIP CHANGES ME

Today's Scripture Reading: Isaiah 6:1-8

As a young seminary student one of my professors required us to memorize Isaiah 6:1-8. You may recognize
that passage as the vivid description of God's call of the
great prophet Isaiah. In the Temple in Jerusalem the
prophet experienced the worship of Almighty God in a
life-changing way; and the same can happen for us.

Isaiah explains in his autobiographical account of
this encounter that it all happened "in the year that
King Uzziah died" (Isaiah 6:1a). It was a time of personal grief and disappointment. Isaiah had lived most
of his life under the reign of Uzziah. Now this man
who had led Israel through some of her most prosperous years was gone.

Was it this grief that drove Isaiah to the Temple of the
Lord for comfort? We don't know. We simply know what
happened for Isaiah: "I saw the Lord seated on a throne,
high and exalted, and the train of his robe filled the temple" (v.1b). So it is that in times of personal disappoint-

ment and sorrow we can experience the overwhelming presence of God in worship.

DISCOVERY

In times of authentic worship we discover things about God and about ourselves. Isaiah "saw the Lord." Was this a vision or a literal appearance of God in the Temple? Again, we don't know. We simply know it was something very real and personal for Isaiah. So should times of worship be for us.

Isaiah discovered amazing things about God. God is "seated on a throne." Our great God and King is at the control center of the universe sovereignly ruling over all things … *all* things.

I once heard someone say that they handle disappointments by changing just one letter in the word "disappointments. Change the "d" to an "H" and you have "His appointments." God orchestrates all things for His glory and for the good of His people.

So in this time of life-changing worship Isaiah discovered that God was enthroned in heaven. The Lord was also enhanced in splendor. God was "high and exalted, and the train of his robe filled the temple" (v.1b). No scene of earthly royalty could compare to this.

The Lord was also encircled with servants. Isaiah saw that "above him were seraphs, each with six wings…"

(v.2). These seraphs are a high order of angelic beings assigned the task of ministering to the Lord of Hosts.

Isaiah also discovered that the Lord was entitled to praise. The angels "were calling to one another: 'Holy, holy, holy is the Lord Almighty; the whole earth is full of his glory'" (v.3). In our language superlatives are expressed by holy, holier, holiest. In the Hebrew language superlatives are expressed by repetition. "Holy" repeated three times indicates the ultimate in holiness for which God deserves the ultimate praise. The fourth verse shows all of heaven reflecting the overwhelming holiness of God.

So in this time of life-changing worship Isaiah discovered something about God. He also discovered something about himself. Having seen God for who He is, Isaiah then sees himself for who he is. "'Woe to me!' I cried. 'I am ruined! For I am a man of unclean lips, and I live among a people of unclean lips, and my eyes have seen the King, the Lord Almighty'" (v.5). In the white light of the presence of God we see ourselves as we are. All pride is dispelled. When you see a person pridefully strutting around you see a person who hasn't seen God. Who can truly understand the awesome holiness of God without being broken to the point of crying, "I am ruined. I am unclean." In that sorry state we cast ourselves on the grace and mercy of God.

CLEANSING

Life-changing worship is a time of discovery, but also a time of cleansing. It was so for Isaiah. "Then one of the seraphs flew to me with a live coal in his hand, which he had taken with tongs from the altar. With it he touched my mouth and said, 'See, this has touched your lips; your guilt is taken away and your sin atoned for'" (vv.6-7).

This is a powerful scene. The altar spoken of here is that altar upon which the animal sacrifices were burned for the atonement of the sins of Israel. There was left a bed of white hot coals from which the angel takes a single coal bringing it to touch the lips of Isaiah.

Now we might ask why the angel touched the lips of Isaiah with the coal. It was the very place where Isaiah needed cleansing the most. Isaiah had confessed that he was a man of unclean lips. What a beautiful picture! The very place where the sin was greatest is where the coal of cleansing was applied. When you and I are honest in confessing our sin to the Lord the Bible says that He is faithful and just to forgive us and to cleanse us of all unrighteousness (I John 1:9).

How reassuring it must have been for Isaiah to hear those words, "Your guilt is taken away and your sin atoned for."

COMMISSIONING

Having seen the glory of God and experienced the cleansing of God we do not have the luxury of just sitting around and twiddling our thumbs. We are saved to serve, not sit. We become a clean vessel that God now wants to use.

So it was with Isaiah. The experience of life-changing worship comes to a climax for Isaiah when he hears the voice of the Lord saying, "Whom shall I send? And who will go for us?" (v.8). The nation of Israel needed a word from the Lord. It's as if in this time of worship Isaiah overhears the conversation going on in the Trinity (note the use of the plural "us" in referencing the Lord). Isaiah senses the heart of God for His rebellious people. And when we truly worship in this fashion we will feel the same redemptive heartbeat of God for lost humanity.

I like to imagine that Isaiah is caught up in this vision of a questioning God: "Whom shall I send ... who will go for us?" Isaiah looks around and there is no one responding. Perhaps he jumps up like an excited school child in response to a teacher's question: "Oh, oh, I know! I know! Here I am. Send me!"

Isaiah's first response is, "Here I am." Isaiah doesn't just say, "Send me!" That would be presumptive. God may or may not choose him for the task; that is the prerogative of God. True, life-changing worship reaches its proper conclusion with the worshipper offering their very lives to

God for whatever He might choose to do through them.

The focus of worship, private or public, is not on what makes me feel good. True worship will be life-changing. As someone has observed, in worship it's not a matter of how high you jump but a matter of how straight you walk. When I have experienced the Lord the way Isaiah experienced the Lord, the only appropriate response is total surrender.

Reading further into Isaiah 6 we learn that the assignment God had for Isaiah was going to be extremely difficult. He would encounter great opposition; his message would fall on calloused hearts, dull ears and closed eyes (v.10). No matter, however, Isaiah would be faithful to the call because he had experienced God so profoundly and personally in life-changing worship.

I often catch myself just coasting through a worship experience or through my time alone with God in His Word. How could I approach the great God of the universe with such a lackadaisical attitude? Why am I not filled with the same wonder that gripped the prophet Isaiah when he had the awesome vision of God?

It helps me to remember that, whether I realize it or not, when I gather with God's people on the Lord's Day for worship I am coming into the presence of a holy God. That should shake me to my core. Every time I open my Bible to read, whether I realize it or not, I am having an encounter with a holy God. I should be filled with awe and wonder.

Back to my seminary class assignment to memorize

Isaiah 6:1-8. I remember walking around the campus with my note cards working on memorizing that passage. Something strange, however, happened for me. The exercise ceased being a class assignment and it became a life-changing experience of worship.

Take Away for Today: Is your public and private worship of God so real that your life is actually changed as a result? The way to insure that happens is to come before God each day with absolute abandon to His will. That is the highest worship we can offer to Him.

PART VIII
ENVISION ... BUILDING CHRIST-CENTERED RELATIONSHIPS

ENVISION: You live as a follower of Christ in your family resulting in healthy relationships, a strong marriage and effective parenting. You regularly experience the love of God and the ministry of the Holy Spirit through fellowship with other believers. You are an active part of a Christ-centered small group where you build relationships that result in mutual growth, encouragement, service and accountability in Christ. You actively participate in the life of the local church, striving to enrich and maintain the unity of the Spirit in the bond of peace. You are regularly pouring your life into others in mentoring relationships. When you become aware that you have wronged someone, you go to that person to make it right. You work to be open to others. You regularly share your spiritual journey with other believers. Earnest prayer with other believers is a consistent routine in your life.

SCRIPTURAL FOUNDATIONS: John 13:34-35; 17:20-23; Acts 2:42; 4:32; Rom.15:5-7; Eph.4; 5:22-6:4; Phil.2:1-5; Heb.10:24-25

PART VIII ~ DAY 1
THE FELLOWSHIP OF THE THREE

Today's Scripture Reading: John 17:20-26

Hundreds of millions of $20 bills are in circulation around the nation at this very moment. You may have some in your wallet or purse. That rectangular piece of paper is more than a piece of paper; it has real value. You can exchange it for $20 worth of groceries or gasoline or pizza. The value of the $20 bill is not in the paper, but in what it represents. Each bill is backed by the US government as being worth the equivalent of $20. Each $20 bill in circulation (apart from counterfeits) is a perfect copy of an original engraving plate stored at the U.S. Bureau of Engraving and Printing.

The same principle applies in relationships. Human beings are created in the image of God. While we are sinners, we all bear a resemblance to our Creator. Likewise as we relate to others we bear a resemblance to God. The Bible teaches us that God exists in three Persons who enjoy a relationship with each other. God designs and desires that all human relationships mirror the relationship enjoyed within the Trinity.

One of the most mysterious and potentially confusing doctrines in the Bible is the doctrine of the Trinity. This is the teaching that "the eternal God reveals Himself to us as Father, Son, and Holy Spirit, with distinct personal attributes, but without division of nature, essence, or being. [48] This doctrine is vital to our proper understanding of what God is like, how He relates to us, and we to Him. It is also pivotal for our understanding of how we live out our life in relationships with others.

The three Persons of the Trinity are distinct, but no one is inferior to the other. Instead, they are all identical in their glorious attributes. They are completely equal in power, love, mercy, justice, holiness, knowledge, and all other divine qualities.

My purpose is not to give a thorough treatise on this great doctrine, but only to show you how it is the basis for our understanding that relationships are important to us as individuals, as well as members of families and of the Body of Christ. The three Persons of the Trinity exist in powerful, loving relationship to one another ... the Fellowship of the Three. What does that mean for us as human beings created in the image of God (see Genesis 1:26-27)? It means that we are created for relationships with God and with other humans. "Since God is within himself a fellowship, it means that his moral creatures who are made in his image find fullness of life only within a fellowship. This is reflected in marriage, in the home, in society and above all in the church whose *koinonia* is built upon the fellowship of the three Persons. Christian fellowship is, therefore, the divinest thing on earth, the earthly counterpart of the divine life..." [49]

In Christ, the Fellowship of the Three has been opened to all who are in Christ. Christ-followers are forged into a fellowship characterized by the love exhibited in the Fellowship of the Three. This means that the Trinity is the basis of all true fellowship in the world.

I often travel to other parts of the world on mission trips. On virtually every continent of the earth I have experienced this amazing fellowship with others believers. There's something unmistakably real and powerful when I walk into a room of other believers whom I have never met before, and whose language I don't understand, but nonetheless I feel a supernatural connection with them. There is a joy and a love that cannot be explained in human terms. The explanation is that the Spirit of Jesus who lives in me is also living in them. The fellowship of the Three is active in the fellowship of true believers.

John 17 records Christ's gripping prayer to the His Father in behalf of His followers as He prepared for His imminent death, resurrection and ascension back to heaven. Jesus prayed: "I will remain in the world no longer, but they are still in the world, and I am coming to you. Holy Father, protect them by the power of your name—the name you gave me—so that they may be one as we are one" (v.11).

So why does God leave us in the world? And what are we to think of Jesus' request that we become one as He and the Father are one? It is so that we might be one with one another in such a way as to mirror the loving oneness of the Trinity. Why is this important? Jesus prays, "That all of them may be one, Father, just as you are in me and I am in you. May they also be in us so that the world may believe that you have sent me ... I in them and you in me. May they be brought to complete unity to let the world know that you sent me and have loved them even as you have loved me" (John 17:21, 23).

The purpose of this unity in the church is that the world might understand what God is like. God intends for the fellowship of Christ-followers (the Church) to be jumbo-screen look into the glorious love that exists in the Fellowship of the Three. As I write I wonder if that is what is reflected in the typical church. Do our relationships within the church provide for non-believers a glimpse into the powerful energy of love that exists in the Fellowship of the Three? I fear that the selfishness, gossip, divisiveness, factions and cliques in many churches have contributed to so much of the world's rejection of God. Is it that non-believers have been exposed to a faulty picture of God because the Church isn't united in the manner that the three Persons of the Godhead are united? If so, we are guilty of gross false advertising!

The life God envisions for us is displayed in love for

others. "We know that we have passed from death to life, because we love our brothers. Anyone who does not love remains in death" (1 John 3:14). Since we are created in the image of God, we are created with the capacity for love within a fellowship of others. This life God envisions and purposes for us when He saved us is meant to be lived out in the energy of the fellowship that exists in the Trinity. The life God envisions for us (eternal life) is His very life … a life expressed in love. The love relationship between the Father, the Son and the Holy Spirit is the model of the love that is to exist ideally between all humans, but most certainly in the Church. However, sin has marred our ability to relate properly to one another. But in the new birth we are given the Holy Spirit by which we can have a connection with other believers called "fellowship."

Take Away for Today: Let this thought explode your shallow thinking about relationships. God's very life is your life now. It is in anticipation of this that the Apostle Paul prays, "May the grace of the Lord Jesus Christ, and the love of God, and the fellowship of the Holy Spirit be with you all" (2 Corinthians 13:14). In Christ we are ushered into the Fellowship of the Three. The love that continuously pulsates between the Father, Son and Holy Spirit is the love that energizes our relationships as believers … in our marriages, in our parenting, and in our churches.

PART VIII ~ DAY 2
CHRIST-CENTERED FAMILIES

Today's Scripture Reading: Ephesians 5:22-33; 6:1-4

What is a Christ-centered relationship? Simply put, it is a relationship where the energy and dynamic of that relationship is the love of God shown to us in Jesus Christ. "Live a life of love, *just as Christ loved us and gave himself up for us* as a fragrant offering and sacrifice to God" (Ephesians 5:2, italics mine). And it's not just the love of Christ that serves as an example for us; it is love that is resident in our lives because Christ is living in us. The Apostle John says, "This is how we know what love is: Jesus Christ laid down his life for us. And we ought to lay down our lives for our brothers. If anyone has material possessions and sees his brother in need but has no pity on him, how can the love of God be in him?" (1 John 3:16-17).

Let's start with the most basic unit of relationships for believers ... our homes. The love that God has shown us in Christ has to be at the center of the most basic and important relationships we have ... with our mates, our children and our parents. Christ is to be treasured in the believer's family so that the love Christ has for us, and the love we have for Christ, becomes the energy by which we love the members of our family.

God wants to use our marriages, the way husbands relate to wives and wives relate to husbands, to show a watching world about Christ's relationship with His Bride, the church, and how the Bride relates to her Groom, Christ. In Ephesians 5:22-33 we find some of the New Testament's most extensive instruction about marriage. It contains the admonition to husbands to love their wives as Christ loved the church and gave Himself up for her. Wives are instructed to revere and submit to their husbands the way the Church reveres and submits to Christ. Paul sums it all up by saying, "This is a profound mystery—but I am talking about Christ and the church" (Ephesians 5:32).

So Christ is to be at the center of the marriage relationship. "Wives, submit to your husbands *as to the Lord*" (Ephesians 5:22, italics mine). So the wife's love of her husband is energized by her relationship with the Lord. A few verses later Paul admonishes husbands, "Love your wives, *just as Christ loved the church* and gave himself up for her" (Ephesians 5:25, italics mine). Again the husband's love for his wife is to be energized and guided by the love of Jesus Christ.

The love God has shown us in Christ is also the example and energy in a parent's love for their children. "How great is the love the Father has lavished on us, that we should be called children of God!" (1 John 3:1a). Dads are challenged to bring up their children "in the training and instruction *of the Lord*" (Ephesians 6:4b, italics mine). This then governs the way children are to respond to their parents: "Children, obey your parents *in the Lord*, for this is right" (Ephesians 6:1, italics mine).

Single adults who look forward to being married can lay the groundwork for a Christ-centered marriage in the future. As you are "in Christ," only date a person who is "in Christ." If the Lord should lead the two of you to get married, the relationships will have begun with Christ at the center.

I think most of us would be embarrassed at how little treasuring of Christ goes on in our relationships at home. I know from personal experience how difficult it can be to talk about Christ and spiritual things at home. Part of this is because we don't see Him as the basis for our relationships as spouses, parents and/or children. One of the great things that can happen in your family is for you and your spouse to see the great thing you have in common is Jesus Christ.

So how do we go about centering our family relationships upon Christ? The Bible is clear that this is to be the responsibility of husbands and dads as they take the lead in setting the tone for Christ in the home. Of course, many homes are led by single parents, often single moms. In that case the mother will need to assume the role.

THE WORD OF GOD

The truth of God's Word is to be the foundation for our homes. Colossians 3:16 says, "Let the word of Christ dwell in you richly as you teach and admonish one another with all wisdom, and as you sing psalms, hymns and spiritual songs with gratitude in your hearts to God." We need to be reminded that this happens at home as well as at church.

Christ-centered families will allow the Bible to be central in their daily and weekly routine. As families regularly read the Bible and discuss it together Christ strengthens the family by His love and truth. Look for ways to make this relevant for every member of the family, even small children.

Above all, the precepts of God's Word should guide every aspect of your home.

PRAYER

Certainly we should pray *for* the individual members of our family. Yet we should also pray *with* them. The deepest intimacy a husband and wife can experience is to pray together. Holding hands and praying out loud together allows you to open yourselves up to God and to one another. Parents, as you pray with and for your children you are covering them with the power, provision and protection of God. You are also showing children that Jesus Christ is Lord over your home.

Reading the Bible and praying together as a family centers your home in the worship of God.

RECONCILIATION

Inevitability family members will offend one another. In those instances the love of Jesus Christ will serve to heal the wounds of offenses that occur within the family. The forgiveness of Jesus becomes the example and the energy by which we are able to be reconciled to members of our family whom we may have offended, or who may have offended us.

CHURCH

The church is an invaluable partner with the home. While God established the family long before He established the church, your family and your church are not to be in competition with one another. Churches should encourage and support Christ-centered families. Families should see their active involvement in a local church as essential to a thriving Christ-centered home. Strong Christ-centered families make for strong Christ-centered churches.

MISSION

Christ-centered families will see themselves on mission

together in the Kingdom of Christ. Husbands and wives should see themselves as partners in ministry in their local church and in their community. Parents should look for opportunities to teach their children the great value of service to others by being involved in the meeting of needs and the sharing of the gospel.

Joshua was one of the great men of God in the Old Testament. He led God's people to conquer and possess Canaan, the land God promised to give to His people Israel. At the end of his life Joshua knew the powerful allurement of the world of false gods and idols. These would vie for the allegiance of the hearts of the people of God. Thus Joshua challenged the Israelites with these inspiring words: "But if serving the Lord seems undesirable to you, then choose for yourselves this day whom you will serve, whether the gods your forefathers served beyond the River, or the gods of the Amorites, in whose land you are living. *But as for me and my household*, we will serve the Lord" (Joshua 24:15, italics mine).

Take Away for Today: Focus today on sharing the love of Jesus Christ in your family relationships. It has to start there. Develop a plan for centering your relationship with your spouse, your child, your parents or some other family member upon Christ.

PART VIII ~ DAY 3
CHRIST-CENTERED CHURCHES

Today's Scripture Reading: Ephesians 4:1-16

Again, a Christ-centered relationship is a relationship where the energy and dynamic of that relationship is the love of God through Jesus Christ. Christ-centered relationships are rooted in the love of Christ. "If you have any encouragement from being united with Christ, if any comfort from his love, if any fellowship with the Spirit, if any tenderness and compassion, then make my joy complete by being like-minded, having the same love, being one in spirit and purpose" (Philippians 2:1-2).

How will we know how to love others? "This is how we know what love is: Jesus Christ laid down his life for us. And we ought to lay down our lives for our brothers." (1 John 3:16). The love that should pulsate in the fellowship of every local church is the very love of Jesus Christ. The Apostle Paul, writing to the dearly beloved church in Philippi, told them, "God can testify how I long for all of you with the affection of Christ Jesus" (Philippians 1:8).

The process of spiritual formation in the church is intended to happen in the context of Christ-centered relationships. Unfortunately we don't always think about our relationships in the church as being Christ-centered. Just stop and listen in on the hallway chatter at the gathering of most churches. Are we genuinely conscious of the fact that we are to be gathered in His Name? Do we treasure Christ to the degree that we are eager to speak adoringly of Him as we gather as the church?

God joins us to His body when we are saved (1 Corinthians 12:13). His universal Church is manifested in countless local congregations. God expects us to be vitally and officially connected with a local church. I have met people who say "I'm a Christian." When I ask them what church they belong to, they answer, "Well I'm a Christian, just not a church member." How ironic would it be for someone to say "I play in the NBA?" You ask, "Really? What team do you play for?" They reply, "Oh, I'm not actually on a team, I'm just in the NBA." That's ridiculous.

The full knowledge and experience of the love of Jesus Christ cannot be experienced apart from Christ-centered relationships in the church. The Apostle Paul had this in mind when he prayed for the church in ancient Ephesus: "I pray that you, being rooted and established in love, may have power, together with all the saints, to grasp how wide and long and high and deep is the love of Christ" (Ephesians 3:17b-18). How do we grasp this love? We grasp it "together with all the saints."

Before we became believers we chose our own friends. We had complete freedom in picking and choosing with whom we would become close friends. When we become Christ-followers that changes. From that point God chooses our friends for us when He places us in a body of believers called the church. When we choose our own friends we typically gravitate toward people who are like us and with whom we get along well. If anything goes wrong, we feel perfectly justified in walking away from the friendship. Nothing lost. But in the community of believers it is different.

When God places us in a church, the Body of Christ, we do not have the freedom to simply walk away from relationships when something goes wrong. In fact, God places us in those relationships not just for our benefit, but for the benefit of others. God uses the inevitable trials that come in relationships to strengthen our faith. We will never learn patience, long-suffering, forgiveness, mercy and a host of other Christ-like qualities if we have the freedom to simply walk away from problems in relationships in our church. God puts us in those relationships not simply to make us happy, but to make us holy.

Community in the church doesn't happen automatically. We have to work hard at it. People join and attend a church for years and still feel lonely. They are missing Christ-centered relationships. Many people are on a quest for the perfect church. "Perfect" is defined by whether or not that relationship happens to meet their needs. If it doesn't they hop from one church to the next looking for the right atmosphere where people treat them the way they think they should be treated.

I want to challenge that thinking. It is so prevalent today, and it reflects a gross misunderstanding of why God puts us in churches (and in families) to begin with. Has it occurred to you that the reason God has put you in an imperfect church or an imperfect family is for the purpose of using those imperfections in others to perfect you? Has it occurred to you that God has not put you in a church primarily to fulfill you (though He certainly does fulfill us in Christ-centered relationships), but to use the imperfections and offenses of others to show you more about how Christ has loved you? I'm convinced today that people never learn forgiveness because they bail out on relationships before they have the chance to learn or experience forgiveness. They get their feelings hurt at a church and then go looking for another church rather than learning to express and experience forgiveness in the context of the church they are committed to. Likewise, many married people, when they experience adversity in their marriage, bail out of the marriage rather than growing in their faith by staying in the marriage and learning to forgive and to rebuild trust.

Perhaps the most extensive definition of Christ's love permeating Christ-centered relationships is found in

I Corinthians 13. Love is patient (v.4). How can we express this love unless we're in relationships where people annoy us? Love is kind (v.4). How can this love be expressed if we're not in relationships where people are unlovely? Love is not easily angered (v.5). How can this love be lived out if we aren't in relationships with people or in situations where we have to wrestle with our anger at something that they have done? Love keeps no record of wrongs (v.5). How can we do that if we aren't in relationships where people occasionally wrong us? Love always trusts (v.7). How can we live this out if we aren't in situations where people let us down? Love always perseveres (v.7). How can that be expressed if we aren't in relationships where we would ordinarily be tempted to give up on them? Love never fails (v.8). How can we live that out if we aren't in relationships with people who fail from time to time? There's a relational application to every one of these virtues. So I can only grow in these qualities in the context of relationships.

Brad Waggoner sets the following vision before us: "Consider living in a community of faith, the body of Christ, where fellow believers actually love, honor, respect, and care for one another. Thing about what it would be like to be encouraged, admonished, supported and challenged by other followers of Christ. Wouldn't it be great to hang out in an environment with little selfishness or harmful comments? Imagine standing shoulder to shoulder with people of like mind and faith praising God and serving Him and others." [50]

Take Away for Today: Take a good look at your involvement in a local church. Are you committed to a small group where you can know others and be known by them? Are you a "giver" or a "taker"? Look for ways to strengthen your ties to a local church.

PART VIII ~ DAY 4
MEMBERSHIP HAS ITS PRIVILEGES

Today's Scripture Reading: Romans 15:1-7

Years ago American Express had an advertising campaign for its credit card: "Membership has its privileges." The ad implied that those who were fortunate enough to qualify for this status symbol card also qualified for exclusive perks and rewards – as well as a monthly bill! I understand that today, American Express' most exclusive card is the Centurion Card. It requires an annual fee of $2,500 and an annual minimum spending level of $250,000. The card also grants its members 24/7 access to a personal concierge trained to make things happen, such as backstage access to celebrity events or concerts. Yes, membership has its privileges.

On an entirely different level membership in the Body of Christ has its privileges. As we are deposited in a local church immersed in Christ-centered relationships we gain many advantages. A few of them come to mind:

ENCOURAGEMENT

We all need encouragement. Most of us *get* too little of it from others; most of us *give* too little of it to others. That's why the Bible admonishes us: "And let us consider how we may spur one another on toward love and good deeds. Let us not give up meeting together, as some are in the habit of doing, but let us encourage one another—and all the more as you see the Day approaching" (Hebrews 10:24-25). I'll have more to say later about the "one anothers" of the New Testament, but one of the great things we do for one another is mutual encouragement.

SANCTIFICATION

God works through Christ-centered relationships to accomplish His purpose of sanctification in us. "If we walk in the light, as he is in the light, we have fellowship with one another, and the blood of Jesus, his Son, purifies us from all sin" (1 John 1:7). I take this to mean that the practical purifying of our lives is realized in the context of Christ-centered relationships.

We should live in such a way as to inspire the best in others. This means that we will refrain from doing anything that offends or weakens the conscience of a brother or sister in Christ. "If your brother is distressed because of what you eat, you are no longer acting in love. Do not by

your eating destroy your brother for whom Christ died"
(Romans 14:15)

WORSHIP

Authentic worship happens in the midst of Christ-centered relationships. Jesus promised "Where two or three come together in my name, there am I with them" (Matthew 18:20). As we gather for the purposes of Christ we may expect His glorious presence. Of course this infuses our worship with great power.

The Apostle Paul prayed for the church in Rome: "May the God who gives endurance and encouragement give you a spirit of unity among yourselves as you follow Christ Jesus, so that with one heart and mouth you may glorify the God and Father of our Lord Jesus Christ. Accept one another, then, just as Christ accepted you, in order to bring praise to God" (Romans 15:5-7).

C.S. Lewis was once asked about his experience of worshipping with other believers. One could imagine that this brilliant scholar and apologists for the faith of Jesus Christ would have a hard time fitting into a local church with mere "mortals." Indeed, such was the case in the beginning: "I very much disliked their hymns, which I considered to be firth-rate poems set to sixth-rate music. But as I went on, I saw the great merit of it all ... and gradually my conceit began peeling off. I realized that the sixth-rate hymns were, nevertheless, being sung with devotion and benefit by an old saint in elastic-side boots in the opposite pew and I wasn't fit to clean those boots. Worshipping together gets us out of our solitary conceit." [51]

PRAYER

The Book of Acts gives us a glimpse into the prayer life of the early church: "They devoted themselves to the apostles' teaching and to the fellowship, to the breaking of bread *and to prayer*" (Acts 2:42, italics mine). On one occasion the church was meeting for earnest prayer and, "after they prayed, the place where they were meeting was shaken. And they were all filled with the Holy Spirit and spoke the word of God boldly" (Acts 4:31).

There is great power in praying in tandem with other believers. Jesus promised, "I tell you that if two of you on earth agree about anything you ask for, it will be done for you by my Father in heaven" (Matthew 18:19). Don't miss out on the great authority that comes by praying with other believers.

PROVISION

The early church provides us a tremendous model for how Christ-centered relationships benefit believers in terms of practical provision. Luke records in Acts 2:44-45 that, "All the believers were together and had everything in common. Selling their possessions and goods, they gave to anyone as he had need."

Years ago I was serving alongside a fellow pastor in Mexico on a short-term mission trip. The church had about five hundred members. One day the pastor brought some of his leaders together to share with me their vision for their church. They realized that transportation was a real need in the large city where the church was located. In the church there were a total of eight cars. That's right! In a church of several hundred only eight families were wealthy enough to own a car, but each of those eight cars was at the disposal of any member of the church at any time. If someone needed a ride to the hospital or to visit a needy relative or any other need that required transportation, those eight cars were at their disposal. That's exactly what Luke had in mind when he said that in the early church "all the believers were together and had everything in common."

PROTECTION

Apart from Christ-centered relationships we are vulnerable to falling prey to Satan. The Bible likens him to a roaring lion seeking to devour anyone he can. In the wild of nature a lion will often look for the weakest in, say, a herd of antelope. That weak one may lag behind and become separated from the rest of the herd. When that happens, the animal is easy prey for the lion. Such is the case for believers. Separated from the life of the congregation we are vulnerable to the vicious attacks of the Evil One. That's why the writer of Hebrews exhorts us: "Let us not give up meeting together, as some are in the habit of doing, but let us encourage one another—and all the more as you see the Day approaching" (Hebrews 10:25).

The German pastor and martyr, Dietrich Bonhoeffer, cautions us: "Let him who cannot be alone beware of community... Let him who is not in community beware of being alone... Each by itself has profound perils and pitfalls. One who wants fellowship without solitude plunges into the void of words and feelings, and the one who seeks solitude without fellowship perishes in the abyss of vanity, self-infatuation and despair." [52]

MISSION

Our mission as followers of Jesus is not to be accomplished by ourselves alone. We do this in community with others. Jesus, before His ascension to the right hand of the Father in heaven, instructed His disciples: "You will receive power when the Holy Spirit comes on you; and you will be my witnesses in Jerusalem, and in all Judea and Samaria, and to the ends of the earth" (Acts 1:8). The "you" is plural. We are to accomplish our mission connected together in Christ-centered relationships.

Take Away for Today: Every church should supply a structure whereby believers are encouraged to regularly meet with other believers for the purpose of living out Christ-centered relationships. Every believer should take responsibility for connecting with a small group of believers for the purpose of experiencing the true Christ-life in community.

PART VIII ~ DAY 5
THE "ONE ANOTHERS"

Today's Scripture Reading: Romans 12:9-21

Christ's love *for* us gives us the motivation to love others. Christ's love *in* us gives us the ability to love others. Christ's love *through* us gives us the way to love others. The life God envisions for us cannot be lived in isolation. God by His very nature shows us that life is to be lived in community. "Dear friends, since God so loved us, we also ought to love one another" (1 John 4:11).

The letters that make up most of the New Testament contain several instructions for relationships in the church, and in Christ-centered families. These have been called the "One Anothers" of the Bible. One writer has identified as many as thirty-five such statements in the New Testament. Consider some of them:

"Be devoted to one another in brotherly love. Honor one another above yourselves" (Romans 12:10).

The New American Standard Bible translates the last words of that verse, "give preference to one another." "Loving one another means we yield our preferences, comfort, goals, security, money, energy, or time for the benefit of someone else." [53] We must take the initiative to find out the needs and preferences of others. It means that we give way and yield to others for the purpose of loving them. It means that we are others-focused rather than being self-focused.

One of the greatest acts of love and respect we can show to another human being is to listen to them. That simple act acknowledges that we value the one before us who is speaking to us. We must focus on the person who is speaking, truly listening to what they are saying (and perhaps even to what they are *not* saying). Then and only then will we be able to speak words that are fitting, edifying and God-honoring.

I remember reading somewhere that President Jimmy Carter made it a habit to focus on the person before him as though that person were the only person in the room. Giving his full attention to that individual helped him to respect and to listen to that person.

"Accept one another, then, just as Christ accepted you, in order to bring praise to God" (Romans 15:7).

I love Don McMinn's description of the acceptance Christ showed to others: "The ministry of Jesus was predicated upon accepting people. He erased the artificial boundaries of culture and status, looked beyond people's sin, and accepted people. He touched lepers, ate with sinners, visited the homes of tax collectors, and washed the feet of the betrayer. Through these countless loving acts, Jesus made a clear statement: 'Never will I withhold my love from you; there will never be a time or circumstance when I will refuse to love you.' It was as though barriers didn't exist." [54] Let's open our eyes, our hearts and our hands to the needs of others around us.

"Greet one another with a holy kiss" (Romans 16:16a).

While most churches don't observe the ancient practice of the "holy kiss," however we do it, a warm greeting communicates that we are genuinely glad to see someone. It is the way by which we acknowledge the presence (and the value) of others. It speaks of openness toward those who are before us. Stop to think about what is communicated when you fail to greet someone, or do so in a half-hearted way.

"Therefore encourage one another and build each other up, just as in fact you are doing" (1 Thessalonians 5:11).

Everyone needs and appreciates encouragement, even if they don't admit it. Encouragement requires that we are focused on what God is doing in the lives of others. God has spoken to me more through the encouraging words of friends than just about any other way aside from in the Scriptures. We do well to remember the instruction of Scripture: "Do not let any unwholesome talk come out of your mouths, but only what is helpful for building others up according to their needs, that it may benefit those who listen" (Ephesians 4:29).

"(God) comforts us in all our troubles, so that we can comfort those in any trouble with the comfort we ourselves have received from God" (2 Corinthians 1:4).

Comfort is needed when there is any kind of loss that causes grief … the loss of a mate to death or divorce, the loss of a job, the loss of health, the loss of hope. To comfort others means that we need to attempt to feel with them … to weep with those who weep. I'm not talking about manufactured feeling, but an honest attempt to feel what another person is feeling. Then we come alongside that hurting person with words and deeds that communicate our support for them.

"Carry each other's burdens, and in this way you will fulfill the law of Christ" (Galatians 6:2).

Burdens can take various forms. When there's a physical burden we can lend a helping hand. When there is a mental burden we can listen as they talk through their dilemma. When there's an emotional burden we can pray for and with them. Ultimately we must all carry the load that God's providence places upon us (Galatians 6:5). God is also good to bring people around us who take the load off our shoulders for a bit, enabling us to catch our breath and continue on in the journey of life.

"Be kind and compassionate to one another, forgiving each other, just as in Christ God forgave you" (Ephesians 4:32).

Kindness and compassion toward others boils down to forgiveness. When we forgive we are set free from anger. When we forgive, and others forgive us, relationships are healed. Forgiveness is a means of showing grace to others ... giving someone else what they don't necessarily deserve in the way of blessing or help.

"Let the word of Christ dwell in you richly as you teach and admonish one another with all wisdom..." (Colossians 3:16a).

Admonishing means we lovingly confront others with truth of God's Word. We need to love others enough to confront them when they are living in sin or headed toward a sinful collapse. We need to caution others when we see them stepping precariously close to danger.

"And pray in the Spirit on all occasions with all kinds of prayers and requests. With this in mind, be alert and always keep on praying for all the saints" (Ephesians 6:18).

One of the great duties we have as believers is to be continuously alert to the opportunities to pray for and lift up others. The Holy Spirit will prompt us when others need prayer and encouragement. The intercession called for by the New Testament is all-encompassing.

"And let us consider how we may spur one another on toward love and good deeds" (Hebrews 10:24).

There's something about the way God has created us as humans that makes us more responsive when we are accountable to others. We tend not to do as well when we are left to our own motivations. If, however, you throw in some encouragement and accountability, we are more inclined to live up to our commitments.

A great example comes from the life of Jean Nidetch. An article in *USA Today* chronicled her amazing story. Despite an endless string of diets Jean's waistline continued to expand through her childhood, teenage and young adult years. She tried all sorts of gimmicks and pills, some of which resulted in short-term weight loss. Then she would quickly gain back the pounds she had shed.

Jean never gave up. In 1961 Jean, age 38, joined a dieting group sponsored by the New York City Board of Health. She started off great. Ten weeks into the program she had lost 20 pounds ... but her motivation was waning. Jean came to the realization that she was attempting this on her own; she needed a partner ... someone to talk to.

Jean couldn't persuade any of her friends to make the long trip to Manhattan for the program, so she took matters into her own hands. She adapted the health department's weight loss program into something that she and her friends could do together in their hometown of Queens.

It was in one of those first meetings that the organization known as Weight Watchers was born. Today it has the reputation of being one of the most effective weight-loss programs anywhere. Jean Nidetch hit on the simple approach that shedding pounds requires more than just a diet ... it also requires support from others.

So the typical Weight Watchers meeting involves weight check-ins. The setting of goals is encouraged for the purpose of accountability. Participants are also coached through open conversation about the challenges, defeats and victories in weight-loss.

At the age of 86, Jean Nidetch said she never told anyone he needed to lose weight. "I don't believe in telling people. But people say to me, 'I wish I could lose weight.' I say, 'Wishing won't do it. I know you can. If you want me to, I'll help.'"[55]

This story illustrates a powerful reality for Christ-followers. We are born again into a Body, the Body of Christ. As "body-parts" we can't properly function disconnected from other parts of the body. Pull your heart out of your chest and lay it on the table; see how long it functions.

This kind of accountability only happens in the context of close, Christ-centered relationships. It starts in our homes where as Christian husbands, wives, fathers, mothers, sons and daughters we submit our lives to each other. Beyond that it helps to have some close brothers or sisters in Christ with whom we can share our goals, our challenges, our defeats and our victories.

Take Away for Today: There is grave danger in a believer living life closed off to other believers. There is unimaginable strength in a believer living a life opened up to accountability of others who love us in Christ. Is there someone like that in your life?

Conclusion

Jesus understands our propensity to obsess over the things of this world. He confronted this tendency in the lives of His first followers with these words: "So do not worry, saying, 'What shall we eat?' or 'What shall we drink?' or 'What shall we wear?' For the pagans run after all these things, and your heavenly Father knows that you need them. But seek first his kingdom and his righteousness, and all these things will be given to you as well" (Matthew 6:31-33).

It seems that most of our energies each day are consumed with desires that relate to the needs of our physical existence here in this life. Stop to think about how your life is typically ordered around where or when you will eat your next meal, or what you will wear, or how you will satisfy one desire or another (some of them sinful).

Consequently, many of us have grown up in a church culture in which we have been taught to deny desires. Desire is *undesirable*. And on the surface that seems to be right on target. However, there is another way of looking at this matter of desire. Perhaps the greater problem for us is not the presence of desire in our lives, but rather the weakness of the desire in our lives. Could it be that God is not teaching us to desire *less*, but really to desire *more?* If so, then Jesus' challenge to His disciples in Matthew 6:31-33 is a challenge to not be so easily satisfied.

The great apologist C.S. Lewis, in his book *The Weight of Glory*, explains this well: "Indeed, if we consider the unblushing promises of reward and the staggering nature of the rewards promised in the Gospels, it would seem that Our Lord finds our desires, not too strong, but too weak. We are half-hearted creatures, fooling about with drink and sex and ambition when infinite joy is offered us, like an ignorant child who wants to go on making mud pies in a slum because he cannot imagine what is meant by the offer of a holiday at the sea. We are far too easily pleased ... At present we are on the outside of the world, the wrong side of the door. We discern the freshness and purity of the morning, but they do not make us fresh and pure. We cannot mingle with the splendours we see. But all the leaves of the New Testament are rustling with the rumour that it will not always be so. Someday, God willing, we shall get in."[56]

The Kingdom of God has come. It thrives invisibly all around us. It whispers to us that this world is not our home. It beckons us to not simply settle for earthly satisfaction, but to fervently press through those desires to the noblest of all desires ... the desire for God, His Kingdom and His righteousness.

Conclusion

The Apostle Paul understood this to be the crux of his calling as he went about the New Testament world establishing believers and churches. "We proclaim him, admonishing and teaching everyone with all wisdom, so that we may present everyone perfect in Christ. To this end I labor, struggling with all his energy, which so powerfully works in me" (Colossians 1:28-29).

This was an all-consuming objective in his life. This objective called for the exertion of every ounce of spiritual energy he could muster as he admonished and taught others. Why? He saw the vision God has for redeemed human beings ... to present everyone "perfect in Christ." What does that mean? It is the very thing that Paul had in mind when he opened his heart to the believers in the ancient city of Galatia: "My dear children ... I am again in the pains of childbirth until Christ is formed in you..." (Galatians 4:19).

"Perfect in Christ ... Christ is formed in you." He's describing a renovation of the interior life of Christ-followers into the likeness of Jesus, so that their outward life would also reflect His life. Again, this is at the heart of discipleship ... of becoming a passionate followers of Jesus Christ.

ENDNOTES

Introduction

[1] Dallas Willard, *Renovation of the Heart* (Colorado Springs: NavPress, 2002), p.83

[2] Brad Waggoner, *The Shape of Faith to Come* (Nashville: B&H Publishing Group, 2008), pp.xi-xii.

Part I

[3] E. Geiger, M. Kelley, P. Nation, *Transformation Discipleship* (Nashville: B&H Publishing Group, 2012), p.71

[4] In Christ Alone lyrics Songwriters: Getty, Julian Keith; Townend, Stuart Richard;

[5] Bill Hull, *Choose the Life* (Grand Rapids: Baker Books, 2004), p.31

[6] Dallas Willard from a lecture at the Baylor University 2009 Winter Pastor's School

[7] Walter Henrichson, *Disciples are Made not Born* (Wheaton: Victor Books, 1975)

[8] George Barna, *Growing True Disciples* (Colorado Springs: WaterBrook Press, 2001), pp.17-18

[9] Waggoner, *The Shape of Faith*, p.111

[10] Hull, *Choose the Life*, p.12

[11] Hull, *Choose the Life*, p.70

[12] Cited in the Pew Research Center's Religion & Public Life Project, http://religions.pewforum.org/reports

Part II

[13] Francis Chan, *Crazy Love* (Colorado Springs: David C. Cook, 2008), p.67

[14] Robert Morgan, *100 Bible Verses Everyone Should Know by Heart* (Nashville, B&H Publishing Group), p.xiii

[15] Morgan, *100 Bible Verses*, p.xiii

Part III

[16] Hull, *Choose the Life*, p.24

[17] Elisabeth Elliot, *Shadow of the Almighty* (San Francisco: Harper & Row, 1958), p.108

[18] Jim L. Wilson, *Soul Shaping* (Nashville: LifeWay Press, 2009), p.23

[19] Wilson, *Soul Shaping*, p.25

[20] Richard J. Foster, *Celebration of Discipline* (San Francisco: Harper & Row, 1978), p.1

[21] Foster, *Celebration*, p.6

Part IV

[22] John Piper, *Don't Waste Your Life* (Wheaton: Crossway, 2003), pp.108-109

[23] John MacArthur, Jr., *Our Sufficiency in Christ* (Dallas: Word Publishing, 1991), pp.256-257

[24] V. Raymond Edman, *They Found the Secret* (Grand Rapids: Zondervan, 1984), p.18

[25] Edman, *Secret*, p.19

[26] Bill Bright, *The Holy Spirit: The Key to Supernatural Living* (San Bernadino: Here's Life Publishers, 1980), p.5

[27] Ken Hemphill, *You are Gifted: Your Spiritual Gifts and the Kingdom of God* (Nashville: B&H Publishing, 2009), p.xvi.

[28] William McRae, *Dynamics of Spiritual Gifts* (Grand Rapids: Zondervan, 1976), p.18

[29] C. Peter Wagner, *Your Spiritual Gifts Can Help Your Church Grow* (Ventura: Regal Books, 1979), p.42

[30] Waggoner, *Shape of Faith*, p.112.

[31] Foster, *Celebration*, p.110.

[32] Foster, *Celebration*, pp.117-122

[33] Foster, *Celebration*, p.112

Part V

[34] Will Metzger, *Tell the Truth* (Downers Grove: IVP Books, 2002), p.22

[35] W. Oscar Thompson, *Concentric Circles of Concern*, (Nashville: Broadman Press, 1981), p.22

[36] Francis McGaw, John Hyde: The Apostle of Prayer (Minneapolis: Bethany House Publishers, 1970), pp.18-19

[37] Bill Hybels, *Just Walk Across the Room* (Grand Rapids: Zondervan, 2006), p.16

Part VI

[38] Waggoner, *Shape of Faith*, p.178

[39] Ron and Della Proctor, *Mentoring 101, Book 1* (Orlando: Campus Crusade for Christ International, 2009), p.8

[40] Andrew Murray, *With Christ in the School of Prayer* (New Kensington: Whitaker House, 1981) , p.121-122

Part VII

[41] Louie Giglio, *The Air I Breathe* (Sisters, OR: Multnomah Publishers, 2003), p.9

[42] David Bryant and Richard Ross, *Christ is All* (New Providence: New Providence Publishers, 2010), p.1

[43] Bryant and Ross, *Christ is All*, pp.6-7

[44] Giglio, *Air I Breathe*, p.49

[45] Corrie ten Boom with John and Elizabeth Sherrill, *The Hiding Place* (Minneapolis: World Wide Pictures, 1971), p.199

[46] Rick Warren, *Better Together* (Lake Forest, CA: Purpose-Driven Publishing, 2004), p.153

[47] Wilson, *Soul Shaping*, p.130

Part VIII

[48] Herschel H. Hobbs, *The Baptist Faith and Message* (Nashville: Convention Press, 1971), p.31.

[49] Finlayson, R.A., "Trinity," in Douglas, J.D., et al., eds., "New Bible Dictionary," [1962], Inter-Varsity Press, Leicester UK, Second edition, 1982, Reprinted, 1988, p.1223.

[50] Waggoner, *Shape of Faith*, pp.xii.

[51] C. S. Lewis, "Answers to Questions on Christianity," *God in the Dock* (Grand Rapids: Eerdmans, 1970), pp. 61–62.

[52] Dietrich Bonhoeffer, translated by John W. Doberstein, *Life Together* (San Francisco: Harper & Row Publishers, 1954

[53] Warren, Better Together, p.20

[54] Don McMinn, *The 11th Commandment* (Irving, TX: 6Acts Press, 2000), p.32

[55] Nancy Hellmich, "Jean Nidetch Shares Her 'Story'" USA Today online, March 22, 2010

Conclusion

[56] C.S. Lewis, "Weight of Glory" in *Weight of Glory and Other Addresses* (New York: Touchstone, 1996), pp. 1-2.